sara foster's
casual cooking

ALSO BY SARA FOSTER

The Foster's Market Cookbook

Fresh Every Day

sara foster's
casual cooking

· ·

more fresh simple recipes
from foster's market

with Carolynn Carreño

PHOTOGRAPHS BY QUENTIN BACON

Clarkson Potter/Publishers
New York

Published in the United States by Clarkson Potter/Publishers,
an imprint of the Crown Publishing Group, a division of
Random House, Inc., New York.
www.crownpublishing.com
www.clarksonpotter.com

Clarkson N. Potter is a trademark and Potter and colophon
are registered trademarks of Random House, Inc.

Library of Congress Cataloging-in-Publication Data
Foster, Sara.
    Sara Foster's casual cooking : more fresh simple recipes
from Foster's Market / Sara Foster with Carolynn Carreño.
    Includes index.
    1. Quick and easy cookery.   2. Foster's Market.
I. Carreño, Carolynn   II. Title.
TX833.5.F68   2007
641.5'55—dc22   2006015276

ISBN 978-0-307-33999-7

Printed in the United States of America

Design by Chalkley Calderwood Pratt

10   9   8   7   6   5   4   3   2   1

First Edition

For Peter

contents

introduction

· ·

IF THERE'S ONE THING that continues to inspire me to write cookbooks, it's that more people are starting to cook and that people *want* to cook more. Time always seems to be the biggest factor when people explain why they don't cook, especially when it comes to everyday meals.

When I sat down to write this book, I kept thinking about how I manage to fit cooking into my schedule. Most of the time, I'm cooking on the fly. I might put something in a marinade before work and heat up the grill while I'm on the treadmill or checking e-mails at home. I'll stop by the grocery store to pick up a steak or some fish or shrimp to make a quick light bite for my husband, Peter, and me or throw together something comforting and tasty, like a quesadilla or English muffin pizza, late at night after a movie.

I figured that others are trying to put together meals in these short increments of time, too. The difference is, I know how easy it can be to pull together delicious meals in whatever brief time you have. Having the right recipes, the right stuff in your refrigerator, freezer, and pantry (and some creative improvisations on those recipes when you *don't* have the right stuff) can mean the difference between ordering a pizza (not again!) and being able to make a satisfying meal, even at the last minute. This book is my way of passing along that information.

I think one of the things that discourages people from cooking dinner is that they're still thinking in terms of an old-fashioned model of dinner. For most of us, growing up, dinner always included a hearty portion of meat, a starch, a green vegetable, and a salad. Even for a pro, the reality of cooking such a meal at the end of the day every day is beyond daunting—it's just not going to happen. More important,

I know from my experience at Foster's Market, and seeing what my customers take home with them for dinner, that you don't even *want* to eat like that all the time—or even most of the time. In this book, you'll find recipes for the kinds of food you *do* want to eat—food that reflects today's more relaxed approach to eating. In *Casual Cooking*, salads are meals, sandwiches and quesadillas qualify as a respectable grown-up dinner (or breakfast or lunch, for that matter), and eggs can be eaten any time of day. Even my more conventional meat, fish, and pasta recipes are designed to be one-dish meals, and the desserts come together in minutes—no baking required.

These recipes get their character not from complicated cooking techniques or long lists of ingredients, but from layering vibrant flavors in delicious combinations. And because they're meant for everyday, often last-minute or unplanned meals, they're pulled together from fresh ingredients that are easy to keep on hand: lettuce, cheese, tortillas, eggs, and bread; pantry staples such as tomato sauce and canned beans; and that essential standby of any seasoned home cook: leftovers (even planned leftovers, like an extra chicken breast or steak thrown on the grill for the next day).

This kind of day-to-day cooking allows you to be inventive and flexible, to make do rather than make another trip to the store. To get you thinking this way, I give you lots of ideas for playing around with the recipes. In "Quick Fix" options, you'll find ways to trim steps and time by taking advantage of packaged or precooked ingredients. "Try This!" offers suggestions for varying a recipe to use what you have on hand. And in each chapter, you'll find no-recipe recipes that use some of my favorite improvisational foods, like tortillas, sausage, and spinach.

ten pantry essentials

Having a well-stocked pantry (and freezer, which I think of as an extension of my pantry) is essential when you're putting together last-minute meals. Naturally what you like to cook and eat will determine what's in *your* pantry, but these are the ten items I think *everyone* should have:

1. Extra-virgin olive oil
2. Balsamic vinegar
3. Dried pasta (both short and long shapes)
4. Canned beans (white beans, pinto beans, kidney beans, and chickpeas)
5. Jarred tomato sauce
6. Arborio rice
7. Salsa (tomato salsa and salsa verde)
8. Sausage (in the freezer)
9. Shrimp (in the freezer)
10. Bread or puff pastry (in the freezer)

That is the bare minimum, just enough to ensure there will always be something to eat on hand. Putting together unplanned weeknight meals is a lot easier (not to mention more fun!) when you have a well-stocked larder to work with. Here is my long list:

BAKING SUPPLIES: all-purpose flour, good-quality bittersweet and semisweet chocolates, chocolate chips, cocoa powder, baking powder, baking soda, rolled oats, cornmeal, granulated sugar, brown sugar, confectioners' sugar, pure vanilla extract, honey, maple syrup, molasses, jam, chocolate sauce, caramel sauce, lemon curd.

DRIED FRUIT: raisins, golden raisins, cranberries, sour cherries, dates, figs, and apricots.

CANNED GOODS: navy beans, cannellini beans, pinto beans, black beans, chickpeas, tuna, artichoke hearts, chipotle chiles in adobo, plum tomatoes, broth (chicken, beef, or vegetable; canned or in boxes).

JARRED AND BOTTLED GOODS: olive oil, safflower or canola oil, vinegars (balsamic, red wine, white wine, sherry, apple cider, Champagne), tomato sauce, barbecue sauce, salsa verde, tomato salsa, roasted red peppers, pickles (bread-and-butter chips, dill pickles, cornichons, and sweet pickle relish), horseradish, mustard (many varieties, including Dijon, whole-grain, tarragon, and horseradish), hot sauce, ketchup, mayonnaise, Worcestershire sauce, peanut butter, chutney (mango, apple, pear, and tomato), capers, anchovies (in bottles or tins), olives.

DRIED HERBS AND SPICES: sea salt, kosher salt, black peppercorns, green peppercorns, curry powder, crushed red pepper flakes, bay leaves, basil, oregano, marjoram, parsley, tarragon, rosemary, thyme, saffron, ground cumin, dry mustard, chili powder, ground cayenne pepper, coriander, allspice, cardamom, cinnamon, nutmeg, cloves (whole and ground).

PASTA AND GRAINS: capellini, spaghetti, ziti, penne, orecchiette, couscous, orzo, grits, polenta, Arborio rice, brown rice, jasmine rice, basmati rice, lentils, split peas, bulgur wheat.

ASIAN PANTRY: fish sauce, light soy sauce or tamari, sesame oil, green curry paste, red curry paste, rice vinegar, hoisin sauce, mirin, unsweetened coconut milk, soba noodles, rice noodles.

FREEZER: sausage (Italian pork sausage, spicy lamb sausage), tortillas, puff pastry, sliced bread, English muffins, pita bread, pizza dough, corn, black-eyed peas, lima beans, Crowder peas, green peas, edamame, ice cream, berries (blueberries, blackberries, raspberries), nuts (walnuts, pine nuts, almonds, peanuts).

REFRIGERATOR: unsalted butter, milk, plain whole-milk yogurt, sour cream, heavy cream, cheese (Parmesan, pecorino, Cheddar, Swiss, goat cheese, feta, blue, Brie, fresh mozzarella).

PRODUCE: apples, bananas, oranges, fresh herbs (basil, oregano, parsley, rosemary, and thyme), lettuce, baby greens, arugula, garlic, ginger, potatoes, sweet potatoes, spinach, jalapeño and bell peppers, onions, shallots, lemons, and limes.

Classic Cucumber and
Watercress Tea Sandwiches

Crudité Platter

Pickled Spring Vegetables with
Mustard Seed Vinaigrette

Roasted Vegetable Platter with
Farmstead Cheese Fondue

All-American Artisan Cheese Platter

Simple Antipasto Platter from
the Pantry

Crispy Sweet Potato Chips

Caramelized Onion Dip

Warm Crab Dip

Five More Indispensable Dips
• White Bean Purée
• Roasted Eggplant Dip
• Curried Yogurt Dip with Fresh
  Cilantro
• Roasted Red Pepper–Walnut Dip
• Avocado Watercress Dip

Chile con Queso with Warm
Crispy Tortilla Chips

Toasted Garlic Bread

Herbed Crostini

party
platters

I RARELY SERVE HORS D'OEUVRES to my dinner guests. They're so much work—sometimes more than preparing an entire meal—and they spoil people's appetites. If I'm having people over for drinks, I do want to have something for them to snack on, but I keep it as simple as possible, which is what this chapter is all about. These are recipes for crudités and crostini, chips and dips, that you can make in very little time using few ingredients—many of which you might already have on hand. I give you lots of serving suggestions so you can mix-and-match depending on what you like.

classic cucumber and watercress tea sandwiches

Who doesn't enjoy tea sandwiches? They're so sweet and old-fashioned. Because these are basically just cucumbers and mayonnaise, it's important to use homemade or good-quality mayonnaise from a jar. If you have extra time, use Quick Herb Mayo (page 77) in place of the plain mayonnaise.

MAKES 3 TO 4 DOZEN SANDWICHES

- ½ cup mayonnaise
- 24 thin slices white sandwich bread
- 1 cucumber, peeled and thinly sliced
- 1 cup watercress, rinsed, drained, and trimmed of tough stems
- Sea salt and freshly ground black pepper
- ¼ cup chopped fresh flat-leaf parsley

Spread a generous layer of mayonnaise on one side of each bread slice and place the slices on a work surface, mayonnaise side up. Arrange the cucumber slices in one even layer on half of the bread slices. Place the watercress leaves on top of the cucumbers and season to taste with salt and pepper. Top the sandwiches with the remaining bread slices mayonnaise side down, and press the sandwiches together gently. Cut the crusts off the bread and cut each sandwich into three rectangles or four triangles.

Spread a small amount of mayonnaise along the cut edges of each sandwich. Pour the parsley onto a plate and dip the edges of the sandwiches into the chopped parsley. Stack the finished sandwiches on a platter and cover the platter tightly with plastic wrap to prevent the sandwiches from drying out. Serve immediately, or refrigerate until ready to serve—not more than 1 hour.

VARIATIONS:
BLT with avocado and watercress; Salami, butter, and aged Gouda; Smoked salmon, cucumbers, and cream cheese; Fresh goat cheese with sun-dried tomatoes and arugula; Grilled zucchini, fresh mozzarella cheese, and balsamic vinaigrette; Smoked turkey with curried mayonnaise on walnut raisin bread.

Good with:

These make a nice hors d'oeuvre, but they're also good (and certainly more unexpected) as a light lunch in the summertime, when it's too hot to turn on the stove—or even the toaster.

crudité platter

For catering jobs at the Market, no matter what else we're serving, we almost always start with a platter of crudités. They don't fill people up, and everybody loves them. *Crudités* literally means "raw," but I like to blanch the vegetables; it brings out their colors and flavors while leaving them almost as crunchy. Use as few or as many different vegetables as you like, but be sure to select only the best. This recipe is inspired by a selection of fall vegetables I bought at the Union Square Greenmarket in New York City.

SERVES 10 TO 12

- Kosher salt
- 6 ounces asparagus, ends trimmed
- 6 ounces purple green beans, wax beans, or green beans, stem ends trimmed
- 1 bunch of baby carrots, trimmed and scrubbed
- ½ head of cauliflower, trimmed and cut into bite-size florets
- ½ head of broccoli, trimmed and cut or broken into bite-size florets
- 1 Belgian endive, leaves washed and drained
- 1 head of treviso radicchio, washed and drained

Fill a large bowl with ice water. Bring a large pot of water to a boil and add salt. Add the asparagus and beans and blanch the vegetables for about 30 seconds, until they're bright green. Remove the vegetables with a slotted spoon and plunge them into the ice water until they're completely cooled. Use a slotted spoon to transfer them to a colander to drain.

Let the water return to a boil, then repeat the process with the carrots, cauliflower, and broccoli.

Separate the endive leaves and discard the core; repeat with the radicchio. To serve, arrange the vegetables on a platter or individual plates and serve with the dip of your choice or bowls of olive oil and sea salt.

Good with:

You can serve crudités with any of the dips in this chapter. When we make them at the Market, we serve them with Roasted Red Pepper–Walnut Dip or Avocado Watercress Dip (pages 33, 35). Crudités are also nice with just a bowl of really good extra-virgin olive oil seasoned with sea salt and freshly ground black pepper.

pickled spring vegetables with mustard seed vinaigrette

Pickled vegetables have all the crunch and flavor you want in a snack without being at all filling. I make big batches in the summer and put them in canning jars to give away to my friends. They look really pretty and taste great. They keep refrigerated for 2 weeks.

SERVES 10 TO 12

· ·

½ cup white wine vinegar

¼ cup sugar

1 tablespoon yellow mustard seeds

2 fresh thyme sprigs

2 bay leaves

1 bunch of pencil-thin asparagus (about 8 ounces), ends trimmed

8 ounces baby summer squash, such as patty pan, trimmed

1 bunch of baby carrots, trimmed and scrubbed

1 bunch of radishes, trimmed and scrubbed

6 ounces beans, such as tongue of fire, green beans, or pole beans, stem ends removed

6 ounces haricots verts, stem ends removed

6 ounces sugar snap peas or snow peas, stem ends and strings removed

Sea salt and freshly ground black pepper

Mustard Seed Vinaigrette (recipe follows)

Combine the vinegar, sugar, mustard seeds, thyme, bay leaves, and 1 cup of water in a medium saucepan and bring to a boil over high heat.

Put the vegetables in a large heatproof bowl and pour the boiling pickling liquid over them. Cover and set aside for about 5 minutes, stirring once.

Meanwhile, fill a large bowl with ice water. Scoop the vegetables out of the pickling liquid and transfer them to the ice bath, reserving the pickling liquid. Let the vegetables sit in the ice bath until they're completely cooled and let the pickling liquid cool to room temperature.

Drain the vegetables and transfer them to a large bowl. Pour the cooled pickling liquid over them, season to taste with salt and pepper, cover the bowl, and refrigerate for several hours or overnight before serving. To serve, pull the vegetables out of the pickling liquid, toss them with the Mustard Seed Vinaigrette, and arrange them on a platter.

Good with:

These tangy pickled
vegetables are
already dressed with
a vinaigrette, but if
you want to add
another flavor, serve
them with the
Avocado Watercress
Dip (page 33) on
the side.

MUSTARD SEED VINAIGRETTE

2 tablespoons white wine vinegar
Grated zest and juice of 1 lemon
1 tablespoon yellow mustard seeds
2 teaspoons Dijon mustard
1 garlic clove, minced
⅓ cup extra-virgin olive oil
Sea salt and freshly ground
    black pepper

Stir the vinegar, lemon zest and juice,
mustard seeds, mustard, and garlic
together in a small bowl. Gradually
whisk in the olive oil. Season the
vinaigrette with salt and pepper to
taste and toss with the vegetables or
refrigerate in an airtight container
until ready to use or for up to 1 week.

roasted vegetable platter with farmstead cheese fondue

These smoky and crisp roasted vegetables are the perfect vehicles for the pungent melted cheeses. I often serve this as an alternative to crudités in the late fall and winter. The idea here is to use cheeses made locally. If you can't find local Gouda or Cheddar, experiment with whatever semihard cheeses *are* available. Hey, it's melted cheese—how can you go wrong?

SERVES 10 TO 12

8 ounces fingerling potatoes (skins on), gently scrubbed

1 bunch of baby carrots, trimmed (with about ½ inch of green tops on) and peeled

½ head of broccoli, cut or broken into bite-size florets

½ head of cauliflower, cut or broken into bite-size florets

8 ounces asparagus, stems snapped off where they break naturally

3 tablespoons olive oil

2 tablespoons fresh rosemary or thyme leaves
   Sea salt and freshly ground black pepper

FARMSTEAD CHEESE FONDUE

4 ounces aged Gouda cheese, shredded

4 ounces Cheddar cheese, shredded

2 teaspoons cornstarch

1 garlic clove, smashed

½ cup dry white wine

⅓ cup heavy cream
   Juice of 1 lemon

2 tablespoons kirsch or brandy

1 tablespoon hot sauce, such as Texas Pete or Tabasco

2 teaspoons dry mustard

4 ounces farmer cheese, shredded
   Sea salt and freshly ground black pepper

❧
Good with:
Serve this pungent fondue as a dip with roasted vegetables or like a traditional fondue with cubes of bread or bread-sticks, or with boiled fingerling potatoes.

Preheat the oven to 400°F.

Place the potatoes, carrots, broccoli, cauliflower, and asparagus in a large bowl. Drizzle the vegetables with the olive oil, sprinkle with the rosemary or thyme, add salt and pepper, and toss to coat. Spread the vegetables in a single layer on two rimmed baking sheets and roast them for 20 to 25 minutes, until they're light brown around the edges and just tender but still crisp. Remove them from the oven and set them aside to cool to room temperature.

Combine the Gouda cheese, Cheddar cheese, and cornstarch in a small bowl and stir to mix. Set aside.

Rub the garlic clove over the inside of a medium saucepan and discard the clove. Add the wine and bring it to a simmer over medium-low heat. Add the cheese mixture, cream, and lemon juice. Reduce the heat to low and stir until the mixture is smooth. Stir in the kirsch, hot sauce, mustard, and farmer cheese. Season to taste with salt and pepper and cook, stirring constantly and being careful not to let the mixture boil, until the cheese is melted and the fondue is thoroughly blended. Transfer the fondue to a fondue pot.

To serve, arrange the vegetables on a platter with skewers and serve with the warm fondue for dipping.

Try this:

In addition to the Farmstead Cheese Fondue, these roasted vegetables are delicious dipped in the Chile con Queso (page 34) or the Curried Yogurt Dip with Fresh Cilantro (page 32).

If you don't have a fondue pot, improvise by placing three bricks of the same size (or bowls or cans) in a triangle. Put a lit votive candle in the center, and set a heatproof bowl containing the fondue on the bricks, just above the flame.

all-american artisan cheese platter

Everyone loves a cheese platter, but nobody more than the host or hostess, because it's so easy to put together. I like artisanal cheeses; not only are these cheeses more flavorful but also each has its own story, so the platter doubles as a conversation starter. Here are some of my favorites.

SERVES 16 TO 20

- FLEUR DE TECHE from Bittersweet Plantation Dairy, Louisiana: a triple-crème cow's milk cheese with vegetable ash running through the center.

- HUMBOLDT FOG from Cypress Farm, Humboldt County, California: a goat cheese with a tangy flavor and a crumbly smooth texture.

- WABASH CANNONBALL from Capriole, Inc., Dairy in Greenville, Indiana: goat's cheese aged only 8 to 10 days; slightly sweet with a musty edge.

- JULIANNA from Capriole, Inc.: a semi-soft raw goat's milk cheese aged three to four months with a buttery, slightly nutty flavor.

- PIEDMONT from Everona Dairy, Rapidan, Virginia: a firm sheep's milk cheese aged two to nine months. The younger wheels are sweet and delicately nutty while those that are aged longer are robust and complex.

- PIPER'S PYRAMID from Capriole, Inc.: a goat's milk cheese sprinkled with paprika that is dense and creamy with a mellow flavor.

- GREEN HILL from Sweet Grass Dairy in Thomasville, Georgia: a soft, semi-ripe creamy cheese with a white bloomy rind and a rich and smooth, buttery texture; aged three to six weeks.

A way to make a cheese platter into something special is to serve each cheese with a condiment. Try these combinations:

Cheddar cheese (or another sharp, semi-hard cheese) with tomato chutney

Soft fresh goat cheese with spicy pepper jelly

Blue cheese with sliced pears or tart apples

Triple-crème cheese with spiced roasted pecans

Manchego cheese with membrillo (quince paste)

Parmigiano-Reggiano drizzled with aged balsamic vinegar

Fresh ricotta cheese or fresh sheep's milk cheese drizzled with chestnut or buckwheat honey

sara says

Go to your local farmers' market or cheese shop to find cheeses produced in your area.

Cheese is most flavorful at room temperature, so remove it from the refrigerator several hours before serving.

simple antipasto platter from the pantry

My friend Phyllis loves to tease me about the fact that I buy the "Party Platter" from Price Chopper, the supermarket in Lake Placid, but it's the ideal solution for feeding a crowd of friends between a boat ride on the lake and an inevitable late-night dinner. The platter comes with sliced prosciutto, salami, capicola, and other meats; I add some nice cheeses, mustard, olives, and good crusty bread. What could be more perfect? Below is a list of pantry (and refrigerator) staples to pick and choose from to create your own party platter:

Breadsticks and crostini

Olives (Niçoise, kalamata, Moroccan green, Italian San Remo)

Caper berries, cornichons, and pickles

Marinated artichoke hearts and marinated sun-dried tomatoes

Wedges of cheese (Taleggio, aged Gouda, Manchego, Asiago)

Cured meats (Genoa salami, soppressata, prosciutto, and capicola)

Dried fruit (apricots, figs, and dates)

Roasted nuts (almonds, cashews, hazelnuts, pine nuts, and peanuts)

Sliced apples and pears

Good-quality extra-virgin olive oil

Sea salt and freshly ground black pepper

Fresh rosemary or freshly grated Parmesan cheese

Arrange the ingredients on a large platter or cutting board. Pour the olive oil into a small bowl and season it with sea salt, freshly ground black pepper, and fresh rosemary or grated Parmesan cheese. Set out small plates so guests can help themselves and several small bowls for discarded olive pits.

caramelized onion dip

This is my modern version of the classic onion dip, modern in that I don't open up a box of onion soup mix to make it like my mom did! The onions are carmelized first, making the dip slightly sweet and very rich.

MAKES ABOUT 1½ CUPS

- 2 tablespoons olive oil
- 1 onion, chopped
- 1 tablespoon fresh rosemary
  Vinegar or wine, as needed
- 1 cup sour cream
- ¼ cup mayonnaise
- 2 scallions, chopped (white and green parts)
  Sea salt and freshly ground black pepper
  Chopped chives, for garnish

Heat the olive oil in a large skillet over medium heat. Add the onion and rosemary, reduce the heat to low, and cook and stir for about 20 minutes, until the onion is caramel colored and very soft. If the onion is browning before it's softened, reduce the heat, add a splash of vinegar or wine, and continue to cook until tender. Cool.

Combine the onion, sour cream, mayonnaise, scallions, and salt and pepper to taste in a food processor or blender and purée until smooth. Refrigerate until ready to serve or for up to 4 days. Garnish with the chives.

CRISPY SWEET POTATO CHIPS
Serves 10 to 12

2 sweet potatoes, peeled and thinly
  sliced
2 tablespoons olive oil
Sea salt and freshly ground
  black pepper

Preheat the oven to 400°F.
  Arrange the sweet potatoes in a single layer on two or three rimmed baking sheets. Brush both sides with the olive oil and sprinkle generously with salt and pepper. Bake for 10 to 15 minutes, turning the sheets halfway through, until the potatoes are golden brown around the edges and crisp. (They will get crispier as they cool.) Season with additional salt and pepper. Serve warm or at room temperature.

Try This!

You can really use most any root vegetable for this recipe: potatoes, beets, carrots, or parsnips (the latter is my personal favorite after sweet potatoes).

Good with:

I serve these as I would ordinary potato chips, with a dip, or alongside sandwiches like the Grilled Turkey Burgers (page 68), Grilled Chicken and Brie Sandwiches (page 67), or New England Lobster Rolls (page 71).

warm crab dip

Warm crab dip is a standard of Southern entertaining. Every Southern woman has her own recipe—some, like mine, based on mayonnaise, others on cream cheese or what we call white sauce (béchamel).
No matter which type it is, crab dip is always guaranteed to be the most popular dip at the party. I often serve it with endive spears as a lighter alternative to crackers.

SERVES 10 TO 12

Butter for greasing the dish

2 tablespoons olive oil

1 onion, diced

½ pound lump crabmeat, picked through to remove any pieces of shell

1 cup canned artichoke hearts, drained and chopped

1 cup freshly grated Parmesan cheese

1 cup mayonnaise

½ cup fresh bread crumbs

2 tablespoons Worcestershire sauce

2 tablespoons hot sauce

2 teaspoons Dijon mustard

2 tablespoons chopped fresh flat-leaf parsley

2 tablespoons chopped scallion (white and green parts)

Sea salt and freshly ground black pepper

Herbed Crostini (page 37) or crackers for serving

sara says
Don't overmix the dip. You don't want to break up the crabmeat any more than is inevitable.

Preheat the oven to 350°F. Butter a 1-quart ovenproof dish and set aside.

Heat the olive oil in a large skillet over medium-high heat. Add the onion and sauté for 3 to 4 minutes, until tender and translucent.

Combine the onion, crab, artichokes, cheese, mayonnaise, bread crumbs, Worcestershire sauce, hot sauce, mustard, parsley, scallion, and salt and pepper to taste in a large bowl and stir gently to combine thoroughly. Transfer the mixture to the prepared dish and bake for 30 to 35 minutes, until heated through and bubbling around the edges. Serve warm.

five more indispensable dips

Everyone likes dip. and nothing is easier to make for a crowd.
If you have time, make two or three and offer a selection of dippers.

White Bean Purée

White bean purée is a classic Italian topping for bruschetta and crostini.
I make it often because it takes very little time and I always have the
necessary ingredients on hand.

MAKES ABOUT 2 CUPS

3 tablespoons olive oil

1 onion, chopped

4 garlic cloves, chopped

1 15-ounce can cannellini beans
or navy beans (about 2 cups),
rinsed and drained
Juice of 1 lemon

2 tablespoons fresh rosemary

2 tablespoons sea salt

1 teaspoon freshly ground
black pepper

1 teaspoon crushed red
pepper flakes

Heat the olive oil in a large skillet over medium-high heat. Add the
onion, reduce the heat to medium, and sauté for 3 to 4 minutes,
stirring often, until tender and translucent. Add the garlic and cook for
1 minute, stirring constantly so it doesn't brown. Remove the onion and
garlic mixture from the heat and set it aside to cool to room temperature.

Scrape the mixture into a food processor or blender. Add the beans,
lemon juice, rosemary, salt, pepper, and red pepper flakes and purée
until smooth. Serve immediately, or refrigerate in an airtight
container until ready to serve or for up to 3 days.

Roasted Eggplant Dip

This is a traditional Middle Eastern dip, also called *baba ghanouj*. Roasting the eggplant before you purée it gives the dip a wonderful smoky flavor.

MAKES ABOUT 2 CUPS

Olive oil for oiling the baking sheet

1 large eggplant, halved lengthwise

¼ cup tahini

2 tablespoons chopped fresh flat-leaf parsley or cilantro

2 garlic cloves, smashed

2 scallions, minced (white and green parts)

Grated zest and juice of 2 lemons

½ teaspoon ground cumin

½ teaspoon crushed red pepper flakes

Sea salt and freshly ground black pepper

Preheat the oven to 400°F and grease a rimmed baking sheet lightly with olive oil.

Place the eggplant cut side down on the baking sheet and bake for 35 to 40 minutes, until soft to the squeeze. Remove the eggplant from the oven and set it aside to cool to room temperature.

Scoop the eggplant flesh out of the skin into a food processor or blender and discard the skin. Add the tahini, parsley, garlic, scallions, lemon zest and juice, cumin, and red pepper flakes and purée until smooth. Season to taste with salt and pepper and serve immediately, or refrigerate in an airtight container until ready to serve or for up to 3 days.

Good with:

I serve this dip with the Crudité Platter (page 16), pita chips, or on Herbed Crostini (page 37). It's also nice on a salad plate with Toasted Garlic Bread (page 36) or in a pita sandwich with Cooley Tabbouleh (page 207).

Curried Yogurt Dip with Fresh Cilantro

We make this at the Market to serve with crudité platters and grilled chicken skewers, and it's always a hit. It has so many flavors going on. Besides the strong aromatics of curry, there's the zing of fresh ginger, the heat of jalapeño pepper, and the sweetness of the apple and the chutney.

MAKES ABOUT 2 CUPS

Good with:

Crispy Sweet Potato Chips (page 27) the Crudité Platter (page 16), the Roasted Vegetable Platter (page 20), or Skewered Thai Chicken Thighs with Spicy Peanut Dipping Sauce (page 150).

½ cup plain whole-milk yogurt

4 scallions, chopped (white and green parts)

½ Granny Smith apple, cored and chopped

2 tablespoons mango or apple chutney

2 tablespoons chopped fresh cilantro

2 tablespoons curry powder

1 tablespoon grated peeled fresh ginger (from a 1-inch piece)

1 tablespoon honey
Grated zest and juice of 1 lime

1 jalapeño pepper, cored, seeded, and chopped

2 garlic cloves, smashed

1 cup sour cream
Sea salt and freshly ground black pepper

Put the yogurt, scallions, apple, chutney, cilantro, curry powder, ginger, honey, lime zest and juice, jalapeño pepper, and garlic in a blender or food processor and purée until smooth. Transfer the mixture to a medium bowl, stir in the sour cream, and season to taste with salt and pepper. Serve immediately or refrigerate in an airtight container until ready to serve or for up to 4 days.

Roasted Red Pepper–Walnut Dip

I had this dip, a traditional Middle Eastern spread, at a party and liked it so much I came home and did my best to re-create it. I think this is pretty close, and I *know* it's delicious.

MAKES ABOUT 2 CUPS

- 2 roasted red bell peppers (see "Roasting Peppers," page 79; or from a jar or deli case), chopped
- 1 roasted jalapeño pepper (see "Roasting Peppers," page 79; or from a jar or deli case), chopped
- ½ cup walnuts
- 1 cup ½-inch cubes of crusty, rustic-style sourdough bread or baguette
  Grated zest and juice of 2 lemons
- 1 teaspoon ground cumin
- ¼ cup olive oil
- 6 fresh basil leaves
  Sea salt and freshly ground black pepper

Combine the peppers, walnuts, bread cubes, lemon zest and juice, and cumin in a blender or food processor and purée until smooth. With the motor running, add the olive oil. Add the basil and pulse to chop it. Season the dip with salt and pepper to taste and serve, or refrigerate in an airtight container until ready to serve or for up to 4 days.

Avocado Watercress Dip

MAKES ABOUT 2 CUPS

- 1 bunch of watercress, tough stems trimmed
- 2 avocados, halved, pitted, and peeled
- ½ cup plain whole-milk yogurt
- 1 tablespoon Dijon mustard
- 4 scallions, chopped (white and green parts)
  Grated zest and juice of 1 lime
- 2 garlic cloves, smashed
  Sea salt and freshly ground black pepper

Pat the watercress dry with paper towels. Put it in a blender or food processor with the avocados, yogurt, mustard, scallions, lime zest and juice, and garlic and purée until smooth. Season with salt and pepper to taste and refrigerate in an airtight container until ready to serve.

Good with:
This dip is very rich and thick from the ground walnuts, so I like it with something simple, like the Crudité Platter (page 16) or Herbed Crostini (page 37).

sara says
If you're going to keep nuts for more than a month, store them in the freezer to prevent them from turning rancid.

chile con queso with warm crispy tortilla chips

This is my version of the chile-cheese dip that is the mainstay of Tex-Mex cuisine. It's traditionally made using processed cheese and canned stewed tomatoes and peppers. Instead, I use Manchego cheese, a hard Spanish cheese with a nutty flavor and smooth texture, and fresh roasted peppers, which makes it a little more elegant and a lot tastier than the original.

SERVES 10 TO 12

- 4 ounces Manchego cheese, grated (about 1 cup)
- 4 ounces Monterey Jack or pepper Jack cheese, grated (about 1 cup)
- 2 teaspoons cornstarch
- 1 tablespoon olive oil
- 1 onion, diced
- 1 garlic clove, minced
- ½ cup dark beer
- ½ roasted green bell pepper (see "Roasting Peppers," page 79), chopped
- 1 roasted jalapeño pepper (see "Roasting Peppers," page 79; or from a jar or deli case), minced
- ½ teaspoon ground cumin
- ½ teaspoon crushed red pepper flakes
- 1 tablespoon chopped fresh flat-leaf parsley, cilantro, or chives
- Sea salt
- Warm Crispy Tortilla Chips (recipe follows)

Combine the Manchego cheese, Jack cheese, and cornstarch in a medium bowl; stir to combine and set aside.

Heat the olive oil in a medium saucepan over medium heat. Add the onion and cook and stir for 3 to 4 minutes, until tender and translucent. Add the garlic and cook for 1 minute, stirring constantly to prevent it from browning. Add the beer and bring to a boil. Reduce the heat to a simmer and add the cheese mixture 1 cup at a time, whisking constantly and waiting until the cheese melts before adding more. When all the cheese has been added and is melted, turn off the heat and stir in the bell pepper, jalapeño pepper, cumin, red pepper flakes, parsley, and salt to taste. Transfer the chile con queso to a fondue pot and serve warm with the tortilla chips on the side for dipping.

Warm Crispy Tortilla Chips

There's nothing like homemade tortilla chips. Here are two methods for making them: shallow frying in olive oil and oven baking. Both are worth the little effort to make them.

SERVES 10 TO 12

8 corn tortillas
  Olive oil for brushing the
  tortillas or shallow-frying
  Sea salt

Cut each tortilla in half and cut each half into four wedges.

To fry the tortillas: Fill a small skillet with ¼ inch of olive oil and heat the oil over medium-high heat until it's sizzling hot. Add the tortillas a few at a time and fry them for 30 to 45 seconds, until they're golden brown and crisp. Use a slotted spoon to transfer them to a paper towel–lined plate to drain, and sprinkle them with salt to taste. Cook the remaining tortilla wedges in the same way.

To bake the tortillas: Preheat the oven to 350°F.

Spread the wedges in a single layer on a rimmed baking sheet, brush them lightly with oil on both sides, and sprinkle with salt to taste. Bake the tortillas for 8 to 10 minutes, until they're golden brown and crispy, and season them with additional salt, if desired.

Good with:

In Texas, chile con queso is eaten with one thing—tortilla chips—but I serve it with lots of different things: bread cubes, Crispy Sweet Potato Chips (page 27), Roasted Vegetable Platter (page 20), or warm flour or corn tortillas (see "Warming Tortillas," page 97).

toasted garlic bread

Garlic bread makes great use of day-old bread. It's something everybody loves, and it's so simple—it takes about 10 minutes to turn a chunk of bread into a special treat. I make these in the oven, but you could also toast them on an outdoor grill or on the stovetop in a grill pan or cast-iron skillet.

SERVES 6

3 tablespoons extra-virgin olive oil

2 garlic cloves

6 1-inch-thick slices crusty, rustic-style white bread or whole-grain bread

Preheat the oven to 400°F.

Combine the olive oil and garlic in a small bowl and smash the garlic with the back of a spoon to release the juices of the garlic into the oil.

Brush both sides of each slice of bread with the garlic oil. Gently rub the garlic clove directly over one side of the bread slices and discard the clove. Place the bread, garlic side up, on a baking sheet and toast it in the oven for 5 to 7 minutes, until it's golden brown and crisp on both sides. Serve warm.

sara says

To brown the garlic bread more quickly, toast it directly on the oven rack or under the broiler.

Good with:

This bread is the perfect thing to fill out a light salad meal, like the Heirloom Tomato Salad with Fresh Lady Peas (page 44) or Grilled Steak Salad with Grilled Vegetables (page 54); or serve it alongside any pasta dish or Italian Sausage Soup (page 168).
I sometimes make a meal of garlic bread with a vegetable side, like Broccoli Rabe with White Beans (page 196) or Garlic-Sautéed Spinach (page 202).

herbed crostini

Crostini translates roughly as "little toasts" in Italian, which is exactly what they are. Made from a nice baguette, they're crunchy and delicious —the perfect vehicle for dips. I use different herbs depending on what I'm serving them with.

SERVES 8 TO 12

. . . .

- 1 baguette, about 20 inches long
- ¼ cup olive oil
- 2 tablespoons unsalted butter, melted

- 2 tablespoons chopped fresh herbs (such as flat-leaf parsley, chives, oregano, dill, or thyme)
  Sea salt and freshly ground black pepper

Preheat the oven to 400°F.

Slice the bread on a slight diagonal into thin pieces and place the slices on a rimmed baking sheet in a single layer.

In a small bowl, stir together the olive oil, butter, herbs, and salt and pepper to taste. Brush the tops of the bread slices with the oil mixture and bake for 10 to 15 minutes, until golden brown and crisp. Season the crostini with additional salt if desired, and set them aside to cool to room temperature before serving. These will keep for up to 1 week in an airtight container.

Good with:

I serve these with just about any dip— White Bean Purée (page 30), Roasted Eggplant Dip (page 31), and the Warm Crab Dip (page 28). I might also toss a handful on the All-American Artisan Cheese Platter (page 23) or the Simple Antipasto Platter from the Pantry (page 24).

salad meals

SALADS ARE THE ULTIMATE CASUAL MEAL. They're quick to prepare, impossible to mess up, and they make great use of leftovers. (A little bit of grilled steak or a hunk of cheese goes a long way when it's tossed with a heap of greens.) Another nice thing about salads, when it comes to making last-minute meals, is that they're not going to fall apart or "not work" if you stray from the recipe. Once you start to think outside of the box, you can make a salad with just about any food. (I even toss take-out Chinese with a bowlful of greens.) These salads are all meant as meals in themselves, and in many cases they contain the components of a traditional entrée, like roasted chicken or steamed shrimp.

More important than which particular vegetable you choose (asparagus vs. green beans or arugula vs. spinach) is that everything that goes into a salad be the best you can find. Choose seasonal vegetables and fresh herbs, use good extra-virgin olive oil to dress them, and only sea salt for seasoning.

tomato, cucumber, and feta cheese salad with fresh basil

Tomato, cucumber, and feta cheese are the building blocks of a classic Greek salad, but I give them a different twist, spicing things up with fresh jalapeño pepper and fresh basil. It makes a nice light lunch on a warm day.

SERVES 4 TO 6

2 tomatoes, cored and cut into 8 wedges

2 medium cucumbers or 1 large cucumber, peeled in strips and thinly sliced

½ red onion, minced

2 tablespoons extra-virgin olive oil

2 tablespoons red wine vinegar

Juice of 1 lime

10 fresh basil leaves, thinly sliced

1 jalapeño pepper or cayenne pepper, cored, seeded, and minced

Sea salt and freshly ground black pepper

6 ounces feta cheese, thinly sliced or cubed (about 1½ cups)

Combine the tomatoes, cucumbers, onion, olive oil, vinegar, lime juice, basil, jalapeño pepper, and salt and pepper to taste in a large bowl and toss to mix. Add the feta cheese and toss again gently. Serve or cover and refrigerate until ready to serve.

Try This!

For a heartier meal, stuff this salad into grilled pita bread halves or serve on a bed of rice or tabouleh.

green curry–ginger chicken salad

Green curry paste is a spicy Thai ingredient that comes in small cans or jars. You can find it at Asian and specialty food stores. This salad is best when the chicken has absorbed some of the dressing, so make it a few hours in advance if you have time.

SERVES 4 TO 6

. . . .

- 1 cup mayonnaise
- 3 tablespoons grated peeled fresh ginger (from a 3-inch piece)
- 1 tablespoon Thai green curry paste
  Juice of 2 limes
- 1 teaspoon ground cumin
- ½ teaspoon ground coriander
- 4 cups shredded cooked chicken
- ½ cup golden raisins

- ½ cup shredded coconut
- ½ cup slivered or sliced almonds
- ¼ cup chopped fresh cilantro
- 6 scallions, minced (white and green parts)
- 2 celery stalks, chopped
  Sea salt and freshly ground black pepper
- 1 cup coarsely chopped fresh pineapple

Whisk the mayonnaise, ginger, curry paste, lime juice, cumin, and coriander together in a small bowl.

In a separate large bowl, combine the chicken, raisins, coconut, almonds, cilantro, scallions, and celery. Add about three-quarters of the curried mayonnaise and season to taste with salt and pepper. Toss to coat the chicken and add more mayonnaise, if desired. Serve or refrigerate in an airtight container until ready to serve or for up to 1 day. Just before serving, add the pineapple and stir gently to combine.

Good with:
Serve a scoop of this salad on a bed of mixed baby greens, or make a sandwich on nutty whole-grain bread.

sara says
If you don't use all of the mayonnaise in the salad, use the leftovers on sandwiches.

heirloom tomato salad with fresh lady peas and apple cider vinaigrette

This salad combines two of summer's delights: heirloom tomatoes and freshly shelled peas. Lady peas are a small variety; they're more tender and sweeter than most peas. If you can't find lady peas, you can use any fresh beans, such as cranberry beans or shell peas, including black-eyed peas, purple-hull peas, pink-eye peas, or Crowder peas. In a pinch, substitute fresh or frozen lima beans, edamame, or green peas.

SERVES 6

Kosher salt

1 cup lady peas

APPLE CIDER VINAIGRETTE

¼ cup cider vinegar

Juice of 1 lemon

1 shallot, minced

1 teaspoon sugar

¼ cup extra-virgin olive oil

1 jalapeño pepper, cored, seeded, and minced

Sea salt and freshly ground black pepper

• • •

2 pounds assorted heirloom tomatoes, cored and sliced

4 fresh basil leaves, thinly sliced

Sea salt and freshly ground black pepper

Bring a large pot of water to a boil and add salt. Add the lady peas and cook for 8 to 10 minutes, until they're just tender. Drain the peas and rinse them under cold water until they're completely cooled. Drain them again and set aside.

To make the vinaigrette, combine the vinegar, lemon juice, shallot, and sugar in a small bowl. Gradually add the olive oil, whisking constantly. Stir in the jalapeño and season with salt and pepper to taste. Drizzle half of the vinaigrette over the peas and toss to coat.

To serve, arrange the tomato slices on a platter or individual plates. Spoon the peas and vinaigrette over the tomatoes and drizzle with the remaining vinaigrette. Sprinkle the basil over the salad and season with additional salt and pepper, if desired.

shrimp salad with sugar snap peas

This tangy shrimp salad is even better after the shrimp have marinated in the vinaigrette. It makes perfect picnic food in the spring and summer.

SERVES 4 TO 6

. . . .

Kosher salt

8 ounces sugar snap peas or snow peas, stem ends and strings removed

CILANTRO-CUMIN VINAIGRETTE

¼ cup fresh cilantro leaves (stems reserved)

2 scallions, minced (white and green parts)

3 tablespoons white wine vinegar

2 tablespoons honey

1 tablespoon ground cumin

1 lime, halved

1 garlic clove, smashed

½ cup extra-virgin olive oil

Sea salt and freshly ground black pepper

· · ·

2 pounds large shrimp

2 medium cucumbers, peeled and thinly sliced into rounds

Sea salt and freshly ground black pepper

Bring a medium saucepan of water to a boil and add salt. Add the sugar snap peas, and blanch the peas for 15 to 30 seconds, until they're bright green and just tender. Drain the peas and run them under cold water until they're completely cooled. Drain them again and pat dry.

To make the vinaigrette, combine the cilantro, scallions, vinegar, honey, cumin, lime juice (reserve the squeezed halves), and garlic in a blender and purée. With the blender running, add the olive oil in a slow, steady stream. Season to taste with salt and pepper and set aside.

Put the reserved cilantro stems and the squeezed lime halves in a large pot of water and bring to a boil over high heat. Salt the water generously, add the shrimp, and cook them for about 2 minutes, stirring often, until they're just pink. Drain the shrimp and rinse under cold water until they're completely cooled. Peel and devein the shrimp.

Put the shrimp in a large bowl with the sugar snap peas and cucumbers. Drizzle the salad with half of the dressing, season with salt and pepper, and toss to coat. Add more dressing if desired and serve immediately, or cover and refrigerate until ready to serve or for up to 1 day.

grilled sausage and potato salad with spinach, red onion, and brewmaster mustard vinaigrette

Brewmaster is my very favorite of the many types of mustard that we sell at the Market. If you can't find it, improvise by stirring a little brown sugar and dark beer into whole-grain mustard (see note). With sausage and spinach tossed in with the potatoes, this salad is a meal in itself.

SERVES 4 TO 6

1 pound small red potatoes or fingerling potatoes, gently scrubbed
Kosher salt

BREWMASTER MUSTARD VINAIGRETTE
3 tablespoons red wine vinegar
1 tablespoon Brewmaster Mustard
1 shallot, minced
⅓ cup extra-virgin olive oil
Sea salt and freshly ground black pepper

• • •

1 pound Kielbasa or Italian pork sausages (spicy or sweet), cut into 2-inch pieces
4 cups loosely packed spinach, washed, drained, and trimmed
1 red onion, thinly sliced
1 cup grape tomatoes or small cherry tomatoes, halved
2 tablespoons chopped fresh flat-leaf parsley
Sea salt and freshly ground black pepper

sara says
To make your own Brewmaster Mustard, combine 2 tablespoons whole-grain mustard with 2 teaspoons dark beer and ½ teaspoon brown sugar.

Prepare a hot fire in a charcoal or gas grill. (Or just before you're ready to cook the sausage, heat a grill pan or cast-iron skillet over medium-high heat until hot.)

Place the potatoes in a large saucepan and add water to cover by 2 inches. Bring the water to a boil over high heat and add salt. Reduce the heat and simmer the potatoes for 12 to 15 minutes, until they're tender when pierced with the tip of a small knife. Drain the potatoes, transfer them to a large bowl, and set aside to cool.

Meanwhile, make the vinaigrette. Whisk the vinegar, mustard, and shallot together in a small bowl. Gradually whisk in the olive oil, season to taste with salt and pepper, and set aside.

Grill the sausage for about 10 minutes, turning often, until light brown and cooked through. Remove from the grill and set aside to cool slightly.

Add the sausage, spinach, onion, tomatoes, and parsley to the bowl with the potatoes. Drizzle the salad with the vinaigrette, season to taste with salt and pepper, and toss until the spinach is wilted slightly. Serve warm or at room temperature.

arugula and spinach salad with prosciutto, pears, and pecorino cheese

Think of this as an Italian fruit and cheese plate turned into a salad. It's all about the contrast of flavors among the pears, prosciutto, and pecorino—a fairly common combination in Italian cuisine. Because it is so simple, the quality of those ingredients—including the olive oil you toss it with—is very important.

SERVES 4

. . . .

- 4 ounces thinly sliced prosciutto
- 4 cups loosely packed arugula, washed and drained
- 4 cups loosely packed spinach, washed, drained, and trimmed of tough stems
- 1 Bosc pear, cored and thinly sliced

Juice of half a lemon
- 2 tablespoons extra-virgin olive oil
  Sea salt and freshly ground black pepper
- 2 ounces Pecorino Romano cheese, shaved
  Sourdough baguette, warmed

Lay the prosciutto slices on four plates or a large platter.

Combine the arugula, spinach, and pear slices in a medium bowl. Drizzle with the lemon juice and olive oil, season to taste with salt and pepper, and toss gently to combine. Heap the salad on top of the prosciutto and top with the cheese shavings. Serve with the warm baguette, broken into four equal-size pieces.

warm sourdough bread salad with chicken and pine nuts

Bread salad is a traditional Italian way to make use of a day-old chunk of bread. When I added shredded cooked chicken and tossed it with a heap of greens, it became a well-balanced meal. Golden raisins and pine nuts are a really nice combination, especially if you like a touch of something sweet in your savory dishes.

SERVES 2 TO 4

. . . .

4 cups 1-inch chunks of crusty, rustic-style sourdough bread

3 tablespoons olive oil

Sea salt

ROASTED LEMON
GARLIC VINAIGRETTE

1 lemon, halved

2 garlic cloves, skin on

¼ cup extra-virgin olive oil

2 tablespoons white wine vinegar

1 tablespoon chopped fresh flat-leaf parsley

Sea salt and freshly ground black pepper

• • •

4 cups shredded cooked chicken

2 tablespoons golden raisins

2 tablespoons pine nuts, lightly toasted

2 garlic cloves, smashed and roughly chopped

Sea salt and freshly ground black pepper

4 cups loosely packed arugula, watercress leaves, or mixed baby greens, washed and drained

2 scallions, thinly sliced (white and green parts)

Preheat the oven to 475°F.

Toss the bread chunks with the olive oil and season them with salt. Scatter the chunks in a single layer on a baking sheet and toast for 12 to 15 minutes, until they're golden brown and the edges are crispy.

Reduce the oven temperature to 450°F.

To make the vinaigrette, place the lemon, cut side down, and the whole garlic cloves in an ovenproof dish and drizzle with 1 tablespoon of the olive oil. Roast the lemon and garlic for about 30 minutes, until they're soft and golden brown. Remove from the oven (but keep the oven on) and set aside until they're cool enough to handle.

Juice the lemon into a small bowl. Peel the garlic cloves, add to the bowl with the lemon juice, and smash them with a fork. Add the vinegar and gradually whisk in the remaining 3 tablespoons of olive oil. Stir in the parsley and season to taste with salt and pepper.

Combine the chicken, bread, raisins, pine nuts, and garlic in a large bowl. Drizzle with half of the vinaigrette, season to taste with salt and pepper, and toss to combine. Spread the salad on a rimmed baking sheet and place it in the oven for about 5 minutes, just to warm it slightly.

Remove the salad from the oven and return it to the bowl you tossed it in. Add the arugula and scallions, and drizzle with the remaining vinaigrette. Toss gently to combine, season with additional salt and pepper if desired, and serve warm.

grilled steak salad with grilled vegetables

This recipe came about as a way to use up some leftover steak and vegetables I'd grilled the night before, and I always grill extra for just this reason. If you plan leftovers you can make a meal like this one almost instantly. Even if you're starting from scratch, it won't take long. The key is to grill the vegetables first, while the fire is still too hot for the steak, and prep the rest of the salad while the meat cooks. *See photograph on page 39.*

SERVES 2 TO 4

- 3 tablespoons olive oil
- 3 tablespoons balsamic vinegar
- 1 14-ounce New York strip steak or rib-eye steak
  Freshly ground black pepper
- 2 tablespoons fresh rosemary
- 1 red bell pepper
- 1 small zucchini, halved lengthwise
- 1 red onion, quartered
- 4 ounces baby bella or button mushrooms
  Sea salt

ROSEMARY MUSTARD VINAIGRETTE

- 3 tablespoons red wine vinegar
- 1 tablespoon whole-grain mustard
- 1 shallot, minced
- ½ cup extra-virgin olive oil
- ¼ cup canola or safflower oil
- 1 teaspoon chopped fresh rosemary
  Sea salt and freshly ground black pepper

- • • •

- 4 cups loosely packed mixed baby greens, washed and drained

Prepare a hot fire in a charcoal or gas grill. (Or just before you're ready to cook the vegetables, heat a grill pan or cast-iron skillet over medium-high heat until hot.)

Rub 1 tablespoon of the olive oil and 1 tablespoon of the vinegar over both sides of the steak. Sprinkle both sides with the pepper and half of the rosemary and press them into the meat. Set the steak aside to rest at room temperature while you grill the vegetables.

Put the bell pepper, zucchini, onion, and mushrooms in a large bowl. Add the remaining 2 tablespoons of olive oil, the remaining 2 tablespoons of vinegar, and the remaining tablespoon of rosemary. Season with salt and pepper and toss to coat. Spread the vegetables in one layer on the grill (or put them in the grill pan or skillet) and cook them for 2 to 3 minutes per side, until they're just tender but still slightly crunchy.

Core and seed the pepper and cut it into bite-size pieces. Remove the zucchini, onion, and mushrooms to a cutting board and cut them into bite-size pieces. Transfer all the vegetables to a large bowl and cover them loosely with foil to keep warm.

Season both sides of the steak with salt and grill it for 5 to 6 minutes per side. Move the steak away from the direct fire, close the grill or cover the steak with foil, and cook it for another 7 to 8 minutes, until an instant-read thermometer reads 120°F for medium-rare (for medium, cook the steaks a few more minutes, until the thermometer reads 130°F). Transfer the steak to a cutting board, cover it loosely with foil, and let it rest for about 5 minutes.

Meanwhile, make the vinaigrette. Whisk the vinegar, mustard, and shallot together in a small bowl. Gradually whisk in the olive oil and canola oil. Stir in the rosemary and season to taste with salt and pepper.

To serve, thinly slice the steak and add the slices to the bowl with the vegetables. Add the greens, drizzle with ½ cup of the vinaigrette, and toss gently to combine.

Add more vinaigrette and season with additional salt and pepper, if desired. (Any leftover vinaigrette can be kept for a week refrigerated in an airtight container.)

sara says_____
Always double the recipe when you make vinaigrette. It keeps for up to a week and it'll come in handy the next time you want to make a quick salad.

smoked salmon salad with roasted asparagus and artichoke hearts

This is a brunch favorite at the Market, served with poached eggs. The grilled asparagus is especially good with the silky smoked salmon in this salad.

SERVES 4 TO 6

. . . .

8 ounces asparagus, tough ends trimmed

2 tablespoons extra-virgin olive oil
Sea salt

CREAMY MUSTARD-DILL DRESSING

2 tablespoons Dijon mustard

1 tablespoon white wine vinegar

1 tablespoon chopped fresh dill
Juice of 1 lemon

¼ cup extra-virgin olive oil

1 tablespoon heavy cream

Sea salt and freshly ground black pepper

. . .

1 Belgian endive, washed and drained

4 cups loosely packed mixed baby greens, washed and drained

1 cup canned artichoke hearts, drained and quartered

6 ounces smoked salmon, thinly sliced
Sea salt and freshly ground black pepper

Preheat the oven to 400°F.

Place the asparagus on a rimmed baking sheet. Drizzle with the olive oil, sprinkle with salt, and toss to coat. Spread out the asparagus in a single layer and roast it for 8 to 10 minutes, turning once, until it's bright green and just tender. Set aside to cool to room temperature.

To make the dressing, combine the mustard, vinegar, dill, and lemon juice in a small bowl. Gradually whisk in the olive oil, then whisk in the cream. Season to taste with salt and pepper and set aside.

Separate the endive leaves and discard the core. Put the leaves in a large bowl with the baby greens, artichoke hearts, and asparagus. Drizzle the vegetables with half of the dressing and toss gently to coat.

To serve, heap the salad onto a serving platter or individual plates. Lay the smoked salmon on top of the greens, drizzle with the remaining dressing, and season with salt and pepper, if desired.

Quick Fix:
To save the step of roasting the asparagus, use store-bought roasted asparagus from the prepared food counter of a specialty food store. Or, if you find it easier, steam the asparagus.

Try This!
To make this salad more substantial, add roasted or steamed red potatoes, thinly sliced red onion, capers, chopped hard-boiled egg, and/or bagel chips to the mix. Or serve it alongside poached eggs.

southwestern spinach salad

We serve a different spinach salad at the Market every day. This is one of our most-often requested. It's fairly substantial as is, but if you want it even heartier, toss in 2 cups of shredded cooked chicken.

SERVES 4 TO 6

. . . .

CILANTRO-LIME VINAIGRETTE

- 3 tablespoons red wine vinegar
  Grated zest and juice of 1 lime
- 2 tablespoons chopped fresh cilantro
- ½ jalapeño pepper, cored, seeded, and minced
- 2 scallions, minced (white and green parts)
- 2 garlic cloves, minced
- 1 teaspoon chili powder
- ¼ cup extra-virgin olive oil
  Sea salt and freshly ground black pepper

• • •

- 1 zucchini or yellow squash, chopped
- 1 red bell pepper, cored, seeded, and chopped
  Sea salt and freshly ground black pepper
- 4 cups loosely packed spinach, washed, drained, and trimmed of tough stems
- 1 avocado, halved, pitted, peeled, and sliced
- 1 tomato, cored and chopped
- 4 ounces pepper Jack cheese, cubed (about 1 cup)
- 2 tablespoons chopped fresh cilantro

To make the vinaigrette, stir the vinegar, lime zest and juice, cilantro, jalapeño pepper, scallions, garlic, and chili powder together in a small bowl. Gradually stir in the olive oil, season to taste with salt and pepper, and set aside.

Preheat the oven to 400°F.

Put the zucchini and bell pepper on a rimmed baking sheet, drizzle with 2 tablespoons of the vinaigrette, season with salt and pepper, and toss to coat. Spread the vegetables in an even layer and roast for 20 to 25 minutes, until light brown around the edges and just tender but still crisp. Remove them from the oven and set aside to cool to room temperature.

Put the vegetables in a large bowl with the spinach, avocado, tomato, cheese, and cilantro. Drizzle with ¼ cup of the vinaigrette, season to taste with salt and pepper, and toss gently. Add more vinaigrette if desired.

sara says
Toss salads just once and as gently as possible to keep from bruising the lettuce and smashing the other ingredients.

ten tasty vinaigrettes

Homemade vinaigrette, made with good olive oil, is so much better than *anything* that comes out of a bottle. There are endless variations on vinaigrette, and I'm always playing with different combinations depending on what ingredients I have right in front of me. Below are favorites from the Market, and those I rely on most at home.

Basic Vinaigrette

Whisk together 2 tablespoons white wine vinegar, the juice of half a lemon, and 1 teaspoon Dijon mustard. Gradually whisk in $\frac{1}{2}$ cup extra-virgin olive oil and season to taste with sea salt and freshly ground black pepper.

GOOD WITH: crisp leafy greens, grilled or roasted chicken, grilled or sautéed fish, sliced tomatoes, steamed or roasted potatoes, or asparagus.

Mixed Herb Vinaigrette

Whisk together 3 tablespoons red wine vinegar, the juice of half a lemon, 1 tablespoon chopped fresh parsley, 1 tablespoon chopped fresh tarragon, 1 tablespoon chopped fresh thyme, and $\frac{1}{2}$ cup extra-virgin olive oil; season to taste with sea salt and freshly ground black pepper.

GOOD WITH: fresh mozzarella cheese or cubed feta cheese, shell beans, green beans, pasta salads, or grilled fish or chicken.

Dijon Mustard Vinaigrette

Whisk together 2 tablespoons red wine vinegar, the juice of half a lemon, 2 teaspoons Dijon mustard, 1 minced shallot, and $\frac{1}{2}$ cup extra-virgin olive oil; season to taste with sea salt and freshly ground black pepper.

GOOD WITH: sliced grilled steak, poached chicken, potato salad, or asparagus, or use to dress a sandwich.

Roquefort Vinaigrette

Whisk together 3 tablespoons sherry vinegar, 1 teaspoon Dijon mustard, the juice of half a lemon, and $\frac{1}{2}$ cup extra-virgin olive oil. Stir in $\frac{1}{4}$ cup crumbled Roquefort cheese and season to taste with sea salt and freshly ground black pepper.

GOOD WITH: grilled steak or chicken, Bibb lettuce, or use it to dress a sandwich.

Citrus Vinaigrette

Whisk together the zest and juice of 1 lemon, the zest and juice of 1 lime, the zest and juice of 1 orange, $\frac{1}{2}$ cup extra-virgin olive oil; season to taste with sea salt and freshly ground black pepper.

GOOD WITH: grilled chicken or fish, mixed greens, rice pilaf, or pasta or couscous salad.

Chile Vinaigrette

Whisk together 2 tablespoons apple cider vinegar, the juice of 1 lime, 1 tablespoon brown sugar, $\frac{1}{2}$ cup canola oil, 1 teaspoon crushed red pepper flakes, and 1 tablespoon chopped fresh cilantro; season to taste with sea salt and freshly ground black pepper.

GOOD WITH: grilled or steamed corn, grilled or steamed shrimp, rice noodles, shredded red or green cabbage, grilled vegetables.

Balsamic Vinaigrette

Whisk together 3 tablespoons balsamic vinegar, the juice of half a lemon, 1 minced garlic clove, and $\frac{1}{2}$ cup extra-virgin olive oil; season to taste with sea salt and freshly ground black pepper.

GOOD WITH: mixed greens or grilled vegetables; or drizzle on hamburgers, turkey burgers, grilled sausage sandwiches, or grilled steak sandwiches.

Champagne Vinaigrette

Whisk together 3 tablespoons champagne vinegar, 1 tablespoon unfiltered apple juice, 2 minced scallions, 2 tablespoons chopped fresh chives, and $\frac{1}{2}$ cup extra-virgin olive oil; season to taste with sea salt and freshly ground black pepper.

GOOD WITH: steamed asparagus or snow peas, steamed fish, or mixed greens.

Raspberry Vinaigrette

Whisk together 3 tablespoons red wine vinegar, 1 minced shallot, $\frac{1}{4}$ cup fresh raspberries, 1 tablespoon chopped fresh mint, and $\frac{1}{2}$ cup canola oil; season to taste with sea salt and freshly ground black pepper.

GOOD WITH: grilled or steamed asparagus, mixed greens, spinach and goat cheese salad, sliced melon, or roasted or grilled pork.

Pesto Vinaigrette

Whisk together 2 tablespoons white wine vinegar, the juice of half a lemon, 2 tablespoons prepared basil pesto, and $\frac{1}{2}$ cup extra-virgin olive oil; season to taste with sea salt and freshly ground black pepper.

GOOD WITH: grilled fish or chicken, pasta salad, grilled summer squash, sliced tomatoes, or scrambled or fried eggs.

sandwiches, wraps, and rolls

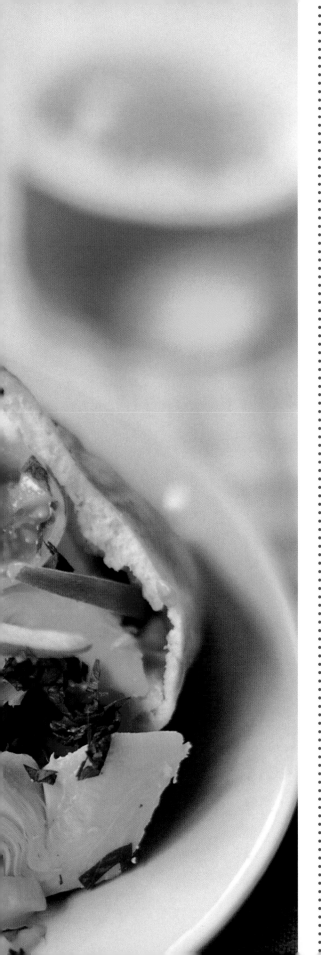

IN MY OPINION, sandwiches are the easiest meals to prepare. It's just an assembly job, and the majority of the components of sandwiches—bread, cheese, and condiments like mayonnaise, mustard, and chutney—require no effort. These sandwiches aren't your basic brown baggers; they're more like entrées between bread. But unlike entrées, there's something about sandwiches (both making and eating them) that just feels relaxed. You can serve them on paper plates, you can eat them on your lap, and you don't need to prepare a side dish to go with them (some variation on chips works just fine!). The best part about sandwiches, is how satisfying they are. After eating one of these, you won't want anything else.

tomato-mozzarella cheese toasts

Cheese toasts are the ultimate comfort food. I like them even better than grilled cheese sandwiches because they're open-faced, so there's a higher cheese-to-bread ratio, and the cheese gets brown and bubbly. Topped with a tangle of dressed greens, this is my idea of a well-rounded midnight snack. (Of course, it makes a nice light lunch, too.)

SERVES 4

- 4 1-inch-thick slices crusty, rustic-style sourdough bread
  Olive oil for brushing the bread and for drizzling
- 2 tablespoons prepared basil pesto (your favorite)
- 4 ounces fresh mozzarella cheese, thinly sliced
- 1 tomato, cored and thinly sliced
  Sea salt and freshly ground black pepper
- 8 fresh basil leaves, thinly sliced
- 1 cup loosely packed spinach, arugula, or watercress, washed and drained, tough stems trimmed

Preheat the broiler.

Brush the bread slices lightly with olive oil on one side. Put the slices oiled side up on a rimmed baking sheet and place them under the broiler for about 1 minute, until they're lightly toasted. Remove the bread from the broiler but leave the broiler on.

Turn the toast slices and spread the pesto on the non oiled sides, dividing it evenly. Top the toasts with the mozzarella slices, then the tomato slices, and season to taste with salt and pepper. Place the toasts back under the broiler for 1 to 2 minutes, until the cheese just begins to melt. Remove them from the oven, sprinkle them with the basil, and top with the spinach. Drizzle the greens with olive oil, season with salt and pepper, and serve warm.

Try This!

Cheese toast is a simple concept that you can adapt to make toasts combining ingredients you have on hand. Try these:

Feta cheese, spinach, and red onion

Cheddar cheese, avocado, and salsa

Brie or Cheddar cheese, chutney, and sliced apples

grilled chicken and brie sandwiches

We've had this sandwich on the lunch menu at the Market forever, and I'm sure my customers would revolt if I ever took it off. Brie is one of those popular foods: anything I add it to is guaranteed to be a big seller. I think this is because it's familiar but also a little more sophisticated (and certainly richer!) than, say, Cheddar or Jack. On a hot day, you can grill both the chicken and the bread on an outdoor grill. Serve slices of tart apple on the side.

SERVES 4

. . . .

4 boneless skinless chicken breast halves (about 1½ pounds), rinsed and patted dry

1 tablespoon olive oil, plus extra for brushing the bread

1 tablespoon balsamic vinegar
Sea salt and freshly ground black pepper

8 slices whole-grain bread

½ cup mango or apple chutney

6 ounces Brie cheese, thinly sliced

2 cups watercress, washed, drained, and trimmed of tough stems

Slice horizontally through the thick end of the chicken breasts and butterfly them open to make each breast about ½ inch thick. Rub both sides of the chicken with the olive oil and vinegar, and season with salt and pepper.

Heat a grill pan or cast-iron skillet over medium-high heat until hot. Add the chicken breasts to the pan two or three at a time and cook for 4 to 5 minutes per side, until they're light brown and cooked through. Remove the chicken to a platter and cover it loosely to keep warm while you cook the remaining chicken.

Preheat the oven to broil.

Brush the bread slices lightly on both sides with olive oil and place the slices under the broiler for about 1 minute per side, until they're lightly toasted.

To assemble the sandwiches, spread four slices of the bread with a generous layer of chutney, using about 2 tablespoons per slice. Place the chicken on top of the chutney, cutting to fit as needed. Top the chicken with several slices of Brie and a handful of watercress, sprinkle with salt and pepper, and top the sandwiches with the remaining toast slices.

sara says

If you aren't comfortable butterflying the chicken breasts, place the chicken between two pieces of waxed paper and use a rolling pin or the bottom of a heavy pan to pound the chicken breasts to an even ½-inch thickness.

Keep a loaf of sliced, good crusty bread in the freezer. Toasted, it's as good as fresh.

grilled turkey burgers with sweet pickles

Turkey meat has less fat and therefore less flavor than ground beef.
It needs the extra flavor and texture these ingredients add. I serve them
on whole wheat buns to keep with the healthy theme.

SERVES 4

. . . .

1½ pounds ground turkey
½ cup fresh bread crumbs
3 tablespoons mayonnaise
2 tablespoons chopped
   fresh chives
1 tablespoon Worcestershire
   sauce
1 tablespoon hot sauce, such as
   Texas Pete or Tabasco
2 scallions, minced (white and
   green parts)

4 fresh basil leaves, thinly sliced
1 teaspoon sea salt, plus extra
   to taste
½ teaspoon freshly ground black
   pepper, plus extra to taste
4 whole wheat hamburger buns,
   lightly toasted
   Sweet pickle slices
1 tomato, cored and sliced

🪸
Try This!

These burgers are
especially good
topped with a
heaping tablespoon
of Spicy Cole Slaw,
page 212.

Prepare a hot fire in a charcoal or gas grill. (Or just before you're ready to
cook the burgers, heat a grill pan or cast-iron skillet over medium-high
heat until hot.)

Combine the turkey, bread crumbs, mayonnaise, chives, Worcestershire
sauce, hot sauce, scallions, basil, salt, and pepper in a large bowl and work
the mixture with your hands just to mix. (Do not overmix or the burgers
will be tough.) Form the meat mixture into four 1-inch-thick patties.

Season both sides of the patties with salt and pepper and grill them for
5 to 6 minutes per side, or until they're just done. Remove the patties
to a platter, cover them loosely with foil to keep warm, and set them aside
to rest for about 5 minutes.

To assemble the burgers, lay a few pickle slices and one tomato slice
on the bottom of each bun and place the burgers on top. Serve with
mustard and mayonnaise on the side.

new england lobster rolls

If you've ever been to Maine in the summertime, you know about lobster rolls and the high esteem in which they are held among Mainers. The simple, mayonnaise-based lobster salad piled inside a buttered, toasted hot dog bun is an integral part of the summer experience all along the New England coast. I recommend you serve them outside in the shade of the summer's sun, with potato chips and bread-and-butter pickles on the side, and in a perfect world, with blueberry pie for dessert.

SERVES 4

Kosher salt

2 1½-pound lobsters, or 1 pound fresh cooked lobster meat

¼ cup mayonnaise

Juice of half a lemon

Juice of half a lime

⅛ teaspoon cayenne pepper

2 celery stalks, diced

2 tablespoons chopped fresh flat-leaf parsley

2 scallions, minced (white and green parts)

Sea salt and freshly ground black pepper

4 hot dog buns

1 tablespoon unsalted butter, softened

4 red leaf or romaine lettuce leaves

Potato chips

Sliced bread-and-butter pickles

Bring a large stockpot of water to a rolling boil and add salt. Put the lobsters in the water, claws first, and cook them for 12 to 14 minutes, until the tails turn bright red. Remove the lobsters from the pot and allow them to cool. Remove the meat from the shells and roughly chop it; discard the shells.

Whisk the mayonnaise, lemon juice, lime juice, and cayenne pepper together in a large bowl. Add the lobster meat, celery, parsley, scallions, and salt and pepper to taste and stir gently to mix.

Slice off about ½ inch from the tops and bottoms of the hot dog buns and discard the trimmed-off bits of bun. Heat a cast-iron skillet over medium-low heat. Spread the butter on both sides of the hot dog buns, split the buns to open them, and place them in the skillet to toast for 3 to 4 minutes per side, until they're golden brown. To serve, place one lettuce leaf inside each bun and top with the lobster salad, dividing it evenly. Serve with potato chips and bread-and-butter pickle slices on the side.

sara says

To save the step of cooking the lobster, buy cooked lobster meat from your local fish counter. It's pricey, but a big time-saver.

spicy lamb sausage sandwiches with roasted peppers and cucumber yogurt sauce

The spicy red lamb sausage seasoned with fiery chili paste, known as *merguez*, is a staple of North African cuisine. I always keep some in my freezer. It's so flavorful on its own that it's ideal for a last-minute meal because you don't have to do anything to it. I usually serve *merguez* with a yogurt sauce, like this one, to offset the heat.

SERVES 4

. . . .

1 roasted red bell pepper and 1 roasted yellow bell pepper (see "Roasting Peppers," page 79; or from a jar or deli case), cut into 1-inch pieces

2 tablespoons olive oil

1 tablespoon sherry vinegar

6 basil leaves, thinly sliced
Sea salt and freshly ground black pepper

4 fresh spicy lamb sausage links (about 1 pound)

2 pita breads, cut in half, or 4 Syrian breads

1 cup loosely packed spinach, washed, drained, and trimmed of tough stems
Cucumber Yogurt Sauce (recipe follows)

Prepare a hot fire in a charcoal or gas grill. (Or just before you're ready to cook the sausage, heat a grill pan or cast-iron skillet over medium-high heat until hot.)

Toss the red and yellow bell peppers in a small bowl with the olive oil, vinegar, and basil. Season with salt and pepper and set aside.

Grill the sausages for 10 to 12 minutes, turning occasionally, until they're brown on all sides and cooked through. Transfer to a platter and cover loosely with foil to keep warm.

Grill the bread for about 30 seconds per side just to warm it through.

To assemble the sandwiches, place one sausage in each pita half, top with the peppers and a handful of spinach, and drizzle with the yogurt sauce.

CUCUMBER YOGURT SAUCE

1 cup plain whole-milk yogurt
1 cucumber, peeled, seeded,
   and diced
1 tablespoon chopped fresh cilantro
1 tablespoon honey
Grated zest and juice of 1 lime
1 teaspoon ground cumin
1 teaspoon ground coriander
Sea salt and freshly ground
   black pepper

Combine the yogurt, cucumber, cilantro, honey, lime zest and juice, cumin, and coriander in a small bowl and stir to mix. Season to taste with salt and pepper and serve immediately, or cover and refrigerate until ready to serve or up to 4 days.

❧
Try This!
Strained Greek yogurt, which is widely available, makes for an especially rich, creamy sauce.

grilled steak sandwiches
with horseradish vinaigrette

Everyone loves a good steak sandwich. We offer this as a special at the
Market, but more often we serve it for catering when a customer wants
something extra nice; somehow steak just seems a bit more elegant
than chicken or turkey. Grilled onions and peppers contrasted with the
spicy horseradish vinaigrette make these especially good.

SERVES 4

. . . .

HORSERADISH VINAIGRETTE
- 1 tablespoon red wine vinegar
- 1 tablespoon prepared
  horseradish
  Juice of half a lemon
- 1 teaspoon Dijon mustard
- 3 tablespoons extra-virgin olive oil
  Sea salt and freshly ground
  black pepper

  • • •

- 1 red onion, thinly sliced
  into rounds

- 1 red or yellow bell pepper,
  cored, seeded, and cut into
  1-inch-wide strips
- 2 14-ounce rib-eye steaks, 1$\frac{1}{2}$
  inches thick, or New York strip
  steaks, at room temperature
  Sea salt
- 4 crusty rolls (such as ciabatta or
  individual baguettes), or 1 long
  baguette, cut into 4 segments
  Olive oil for brushing the bread
- 4 cups loosely packed arugula
  Freshly ground black pepper

Prepare a hot fire in a charcoal or gas grill. (Or just before you're ready
to cook the onion and pepper, heat a grill pan or cast-iron skillet over
medium-high heat until hot.)

To make the vinaigrette, whisk the vinegar, horseradish, lemon juice,
and mustard together in a small bowl. Gradually whisk in the olive oil,
season to taste with salt and pepper, and set aside.

Grill the onion and pepper for about 3 minutes per side, until tender.
Remove the vegetables to a platter and cover them loosely with foil to
keep warm.

Season both sides of the steak with salt and grill it for 5 to 6 minutes
per side. Move the steak away from the direct fire, close the grill or
cover the steak with foil, and cook for another 7 to 8 minutes, until an

instant-read thermometer reads 120°F for medium-rare (for medium, cook the steaks a few more minutes, until the thermometer reads 130°F). Transfer the steak to a cutting board, cover it loosely with foil, and let it rest for about 5 minutes.

While the steaks are resting, brush the cut side of the bread lightly with olive oil and place it cut side down on the grill for about 2 minutes, until lightly toasted.

Thinly slice the steak crosswise against the grain, and lay the slices on the bottom halves of the rolls, dividing them evenly. Top with the onion, pepper, and arugula, spoon the vinaigrette over them, and season to taste with salt and pepper. Place the remaining toast slices on the sandwiches, slice each sandwich in half, and serve.

shrimp po'boys with quick herb mayo

We serve these classic New Orleans sandwiches at the Market every year during Mardi Gras. The sandwiches are a lot easier to make using steamed shrimp, a bit lighter than the typical fried version.

SERVES 2 TO 4

- 1 pound steamed large shrimp, peeled and deveined
- ½ cup Quick Herb Mayo (recipe follows)
  Juice of 1 lemon
- 3 tablespoons chopped fresh dill
- Sea salt and freshly ground black pepper
- 1 baguette (about 20 inches long)
- 4 medium dill pickles, thinly sliced into rounds
- 3 cups loosely packed mixed baby greens or arugula

Preheat the oven to broil.

Place the shrimp in a medium bowl. Add ¼ cup of the Quick Herb Mayo, lemon juice, and dill. Season to taste with salt and pepper, and toss to mix thoroughly.

Slice the baguette in half through the middle, leaving one side intact so the bread is hinged. Open the baguette and place it cut side up under the broiler for about 1 minute, until lightly toasted.

To assemble the sandwich, spread the remaining ¼ cup of mayonnaise on the insides of the baguette. Lay the pickles on the bottom of the baguette and lay the shrimp on top of the pickles. Top the sandwich with the baby greens, close, and slice it into four equal-size pieces.

QUICK HERB MAYO
Makes about 1 cup

- 1 cup mayonnaise
- 2 tablespoons fresh flat-leaf parsley
- 2 tablespoons fresh dill
- 1 tablespoon lemon juice
- 4 fresh basil leaves
- Sea salt and freshly ground black pepper

Put the mayonnaise, parsley, dill, lemon juice, basil, and salt and pepper to taste in a blender and pulse just until the mayonnaise is smooth and green. Serve or refrigerate in an airtight container until ready to use or for up to 1 week.

Try This!

Dressing up bottled mayonnaise with fresh herbs takes very little time and it transforms something ordinary into a special condiment. You can spread this on grilled steak, chicken, or vegetable sandwiches, or serve it as a dip for a Crudité Platter (page 16).

grilled vegetable "patty melts" with spinach and feta cheese

This vegetarian creation takes the grilled cheese sandwich to a new level. It's one of our most popular sandwiches at the Market. I gave it this name because it has the characteristics of a patty melt—gooey cheese and tangy, crunchy vegetables—without the meat. When assembling them, distribute the ingredients evenly within the pita halves so each bite contains a bit of everything. *See photograph on page 62.*

SERVES 4

. . . .

Try This!

Toss sliced pitted olives into the vegetable mix or add other pickled vegetables such as okra, capers, green beans, carrots, asparagus, peppers, or jalapeño peppers. Or beef it up with the addition of sliced ham or shredded cooked chicken.

1 cup canned artichoke hearts, drained and halved

1 cup grape tomatoes or small cherry tomatoes, halved

2 roasted red bell peppers (see "Roasting Peppers," opposite; or from a jar or deli case), thinly sliced

6 pepperoncini peppers, thinly sliced

½ red onion, thinly sliced

1 tablespoon chopped fresh oregano or flat-leaf parsley

1 tablespoon extra-virgin oil olive

1 tablespoon red vine vinegar
Sea salt and freshly ground black pepper

4 pita breads, halved crosswise into half-moons

2 cups loosely packed spinach, washed, drained, and trimmed of tough stems

4 ounces feta cheese, thinly sliced

2 tablespoons unsalted butter

Combine the artichoke hearts, tomatoes, red peppers, pepperoncini peppers, onion, and oregano in a large bowl. Drizzle the vegetables with the olive oil and vinegar, season to taste with salt and pepper, and toss to combine.

Place the pita halves on a work surface with the openings facing you. Scatter about ¼ cup of spinach leaves on the bottom of each pita half. Divide the vegetable mixture evenly among the sandwiches, and lay the feta cheese slices on top of the vegetables.

To grill the sandwiches, melt 1 tablespoon of the butter in a large nonstick skillet over medium-high heat and heat it until sizzling. Place four of the sandwich halves in the skillet to cook for 1 to 2 minutes per side, until they're slightly brown and the cheese begins to melt. Remove the sandwiches to a platter and cover them loosely with foil to keep warm. Repeat, heating the remaining tablespoon of butter and grilling the remaining pitas in the same way. Serve warm, two pita halves per person.

ROASTING PEPPERS

To roast peppers, place them over the hottest part of the grill or directly on the burner of a gas stove. Roast the pepper for 8 to 10 minutes, turning often, until charred on all sides. Remove the peppers from the grill and place them in a paper bag to steam for about 5 minutes to loosen the skins. Peel the blackened skins from the peppers and remove and discard the seeds and core.

grilled focaccia sandwich for a crowd

This is my version of a muffuletta, the classic Italian-American sandwich of New Orleans that's piled high with an assortment of Italian sliced meats and cheeses and topped with a tangy salad. I grill mine; I think any sandwich tastes better with melted cheese. Serve this while the cheese is still gooey, with ice-cold beer and potato chips.

SERVES 4 TO 6

. . . .

¼ cup prepared basil pesto

1 8- to 10-inch round focaccia or ciabatta, halved

8 ounces fresh mozzarella cheese, thinly sliced

8 ounces thinly sliced assorted meats (such as prosciutto, salami, soppressata, capicola, turkey, ham, or chicken)

2 roasted red bell peppers (page 79; or from a jar or deli case), thinly sliced

2 tomatoes, thinly sliced

4 cups loosely packed mixed baby greens

2 tablespoons olive oil, plus extra for brushing the bread

2 tablespoons balsamic vinegar

To assemble the sandwich, spread the pesto on the bottom half of the bread and lay the cheese slices on top. Lay the meats on top of the cheese, distribute the peppers and tomatoes evenly over the meats, and top with the greens.

Mix the olive oil and vinegar together and brush the mixture onto the cut side of the top piece of bread. Place the bread on top of the sandwich, then brush the outsides of the bread lightly with olive oil.

Heat a large cast-iron skillet or griddle over medium-high heat. Place the sandwich in the skillet and weigh it down with a smaller, heavy skillet. Grill the sandwich for 3 to 4 minutes per side, until golden brown and the cheese begins to melt.

Transfer the sandwich to a cutting board. If you're using a round loaf, cut it into four to six pie-shaped wedges. Cut a long loaf into four to six equal-size segments and serve warm.

sara says_____
If you're making this sandwich to serve later, for a picnic or tailgating, skip the step of grilling it and serve cold or at toom temperature.

thai-style sliced beef lettuce wraps

I think using lettuce as a "wrap" is a brilliant idea; you get the freshness of a salad and the satisfaction of a wrap. Arrange the lettuce around the platter of meat so people can wrap their own.

SERVES 4 TO 6

FOR THE MARINADE
- 3 tablespoons chopped fresh cilantro
- 2 tablespoons tamarind paste, hoisin sauce, or barbecue sauce
- 2 tablespoons soy sauce
- 1 tablespoon grated peeled fresh ginger (from a 1-inch piece)
  Grated zest and juice of 1 orange
  Grated zest and juice of 1 lime
- 2 scallions, minced (white and green parts)
- 1 garlic clove, minced
- 1 tablespoon honey
- 1 small fresh red or green chile, thinly sliced

• • •

- 1½ pounds skirt steak, cut crosswise into 6-inch pieces
  Sea salt and freshly ground black pepper
- 1 head of Bibb lettuce or 2 endive leaves separated

To make the marinade, stir the cilantro, tamarind paste, soy sauce, ginger, orange zest and juice, lime zest and juice, scallions, garlic, honey, and chile together in a small bowl.

Place the steak in a shallow glass bowl or large sealable plastic bag. Pour half of the marinade over the steak and turn the meat or shake the bag to coat it with the marinade. (Reserve the remaining marinade for serving.) Cover the bowl or close the bag and set aside to marinate for about 30 minutes at room temperature or up to overnight in the refrigerator.

Heat a grill pan or cast-iron skillet over medium-high heat until hot. Remove the steak from the marinade and season both sides to taste with salt and pepper. Cook the steak for 3 to 4 minutes per side for medium-rare. Transfer the steak to a cutting board, cover it loosely with foil to keep warm, and allow it to rest for about 5 minutes before slicing.

To serve, thinly slice the steak diagonally against the grain and put the steak slices on a platter. Drizzle the meat with the reserved marinade and arrange the lettuce leaves around the platter.

quesadillas, tacos, tostadas, and pizzas

PART OF CASUAL EATING is *comfortable* eating, and what's more comforting than quesadillas and pizzas? They're like grown-up versions of the foods you loved as a kid. I've grouped quesadillas, tostadas, tacos, and pizzas in the same chapter because they share similar qualities: they're all based on the layering of different flavors in delicious combinations; and in making all of them, improvisation is key. I almost never go about making any of these dishes with a specific idea in mind. I'm more likely to pull out a bag of tortillas from the refrigerator or bread for pizza crust out of the freezer, and then start rummaging around for other ingredients—a chunk of cheese, a few leftover slices of chicken or steak, fresh herbs—until I've got a tasty combination. This is why, in addition to the recipes, I give you ten variations for quesadillas and another ten for pizzas. Don't stop there, though; I encourage you to improvise.

barbecued chicken and chickpea quesadillas

The barbecued chicken pizza Wolfgang Puck first served at Spago in Hollywood inspired this quesadilla, which we serve as a special at the Market. The combination seems kind of strange to people at first, but once they try it, they love it.

SERVES 4 TO 6

. . . .

2 cups shredded cooked chicken

½ cup bottled barbecue sauce
    Sea salt and freshly ground
    black pepper

1 15-ounce can chickpeas (about
    2 cups), drained but not rinsed,
    2 tablespoons liquid reserved

2 garlic cloves, minced

2 scallions, minced (white and
    green parts)

8 7-inch flour tortillas

½ cup fresh cilantro leaves

2 ounces smoked Gouda cheese,
    shredded (about ½ cup)

2 ounces Monterey Jack cheese,
    shredded (about ½ cup)
    Olive oil for oiling the grill pan

Preheat the oven to 200°F.

Combine the chicken and barbecue sauce in a medium bowl, season to taste with salt and pepper, and toss gently to coat.

In a separate medium bowl, combine the chickpeas and the reserved liquid, garlic, and scallions and mash the ingredients together with a potato masher, leaving the mixture slightly chunky. Season to taste with salt and pepper and stir to combine.

To assemble the quesadillas, lay the tortillas on a flat work surface and spread the chickpea mixture over half of each tortilla, dividing it evenly. Top with the chicken and sprinkle each with a few cilantro leaves and the cheeses. Fold the tortillas in half to form half-moons.

Lightly grease a grill pan or cast-iron skillet with olive oil and heat it over medium-high heat until it's hot. Place two of the quesadillas in the skillet to grill for about 2 minutes per side, turning once, until the cheese is melted and the tortillas are golden brown. Transfer the quesadillas to a baking sheet and place them in the oven to keep them warm. Repeat the process with the remaining quesadillas, adding more oil to the pan if it's dry. Cut the quesadillas into wedges and serve warm.

Try This!
Serve with Cilantro-Lime Sour Cream (page 96) or Avocado Watercress Dip (page 33).

quesadilla variations

When I make quesadillas, I don't feel compelled to limit my imagination to traditional Mexican ingredients. The only requirement is that they contain cheese—beyond that, I just use combinations of ingredients that I like. Below are some favorites that I make at Foster's Market and at home.

sara says_____
When you're grilling quesadillas, if two don't fit in your skillet without overlapping, reduce the amount of oil you add to the pan and cook them one at a time.

SPICY GRILLED CHICKEN WITH CORN QUESADILLAS
Thinly sliced grilled chicken breast topped with shredded Monterey Jack or pepper Jack cheese, cooked corn kernels, and chopped fresh cilantro.

SWEET POTATO–BLACK BEAN QUESADILLAS
A thin layer of baked sweet potato topped with cooked black beans, shredded Cheddar cheese, and minced jalapeño pepper.

ROASTED GARLIC, ROASTED RED PEPPER, AND BRIE CHEESE QUESADILLAS
A thin layer of Brie or cream cheese topped with thin slices of roasted pepper and raw onion, a few smashed roasted garlic cloves, fresh basil leaves, and a sprinkling of grated Parmesan cheese.

FRIED EGG WITH FRESH HERBS AND SALSA QUESADILLAS
Two fried eggs topped with chopped tomatoes, fresh herbs (parsley, oregano, or basil), and shredded Cheddar or pepper Jack cheese.

PULLED PORK WITH COLE SLAW AND GOAT CHEESE QUESADILLAS
Chopped or pulled cooked pork topped with a small amount of cole slaw and crumbled goat cheese.

STEAK WITH SHREDDED ROMAINE AND RANCH DRESSING QUESADILLAS
Thin slices of cooked steak and shredded fresh mozzarella cheese topped with shredded romaine, diced tomatoes, and a drizzle of ranch dressing.

SHRIMP WITH RICOTTA CHEESE, TOMATOES, AND WATERCRESS QUESADILLAS
A thin layer of fresh ricotta cheese topped with cooked shrimp, chopped tomatoes, and watercress.

ROASTED CHICKEN, SPINACH, AND GOAT CHEESE QUESADILLAS
A thin layer of goat cheese topped with shredded roasted chicken and a small handful of spinach.

FARMER CHEESE WITH SLICED PEARS, HONEY, AND BLACK PEPPER QUESADILLAS *(pictured opposite)*
A thin layer of farmer cheese topped with thinly sliced pears, drizzled with honey, and sprinkled with black pepper.

SALSA FRESCA

Makes 2 to 3 cups

2 tomatoes (or 4 plum tomatoes),
  cored and chopped
2 tablespoons chopped fresh cilantro
2 scallions, minced (white and green
  parts)
1 jalapeño pepper, cored, seeded,
  and minced
Juice of 1 lime
Sea salt and freshly ground
  black pepper

Combine the tomatoes, cilantro,
scallions, jalapeño pepper, and lime
juice in a small bowl and stir to mix.
Season the salsa with salt and pepper
to taste and serve or refrigerate in an
airtight container until ready to serve
or up to 1 week.

pork fajita tostadas with salsa fresca

Beef, or occasionally chicken, is the most typical fajita filling, but pork is just as easy and more unexpected.

SERVES 4

- 1 1-pound pork tenderloin
- 4 corn tortillas
- 3 tablespoons olive oil, plus extra for brushing the tortillas
   Sea salt and freshly ground black pepper
- 1 jalapeño pepper, cored, seeded, and minced
- 1 garlic clove, minced
- 1 red onion, thinly sliced

- 1 red or yellow bell pepper, cored, seeded, and julienned
- 2 cups loosely packed mixed baby greens
- 1 avocado, halved, pitted, peeled, and thinly sliced
   Salsa Fresca (recipe follows)
- ¼ cup low-fat or whole-milk sour cream

Quick Fix:

To save the step of cooking the pork, use leftover pork, steak, chicken, or shrimp in place of the pork tenderloin in this recipe.

Preheat the oven to 375°F.

Trim the fat and sinew from the pork, rinse, and pat dry. Slice the tenderloin into ½-inch-thick rounds and cut the rounds into thin strips.

To toast the tortillas, scatter them on a baking sheet. Brush the tops lightly with olive oil, season them with salt and pepper to taste, and bake them for 10 to 12 minutes, until they're golden brown and crispy.

Meanwhile, heat 2 tablespoons of the olive oil in a large skillet over medium-high heat. Add the pork and jalapeño pepper and season with salt and pepper. Cook, stirring occasionally, for 4 to 5 minutes, adding the garlic during the last minute of cooking, until the pork is light brown and cooked through. Remove the pork to a platter.

In the same skillet, heat the remaining tablespoon of oil over medium-high heat. Add the onion and bell pepper, and cook and stir for 3 to 4 minutes, until tender. Return the pork to the pan and reheat for about 1 minute.

Lay the toasted tortillas on individual plates and pile the pork mixture in the center of each, dividing it evenly. Top each tostada with ½ cup of greens, and the avocado slices. Spoon about 2 tablespoons of Salsa Fresca on each tostada and dollop a tablespoon of sour cream.

grilled shrimp and goat cheese tostadas

With the shrimp and tortillas cooked on the grill, these tostadas are a nice choice for a warm summer night. If you don't want to fire up the grill, you can cook the shrimp in a grill pan, heated over medium-high heat to just before the smoking point.

SERVES 4

- 2 tablespoons olive oil, plus extra for brushing the tortillas
- 1½ tablespoons chopped fresh cilantro
- 2 scallions, minced (white and green parts)
- 1 jalapeño pepper, cored, seeded, and minced
  Juice of 1 lime
- 1 pound large shrimp, peeled and deveined
  Sea salt and freshly ground black pepper
- 4 7-inch flour tortillas
- 2 cups loosely packed mixed baby greens
- 4 ounces fresh goat cheese, crumbled (about 1 cup)
- ¼ cup fresh cilantro leaves
- 1 avocado, halved, pitted, peeled, and sliced
  Cilantro Chimichurri (recipe follows)
- 1 lime, quartered

Prepare a hot fire in a charcoal or gas grill.

Stir the olive oil, cilantro, scallions, jalapeño pepper, and lime juice together in a medium bowl. Add the shrimp and toss to coat. Cover the bowl and marinate the shrimp for about 5 minutes.

Remove the shrimp from the marinade, season to taste with salt and pepper, and grill for 1½ minutes per side, until pink and cooked through.

Brush one side of each tortilla lightly with olive oil, season with salt and pepper, and grill for about 1 minute per side, until golden brown and crispy.

Lay the toasted tortillas on four plates and arrange the shrimp on top. Pile the greens on top of the shrimp, sprinkle with the goat cheese and cilantro leaves, and lay the avocado slices on top. Drizzle each tostada with Cilantro Chimichurri, season with salt and pepper, and serve with the lime wedges and the remaining chimichurri on the side.

CILANTRO CHIMICHURRI
Makes about 1 cup

1½ cups packed fresh cilantro leaves
½ cup packed fresh flat-leaf
    parsley leaves
2 tablespoons chopped fresh oregano
1 tablespoon honey
2 garlic cloves
½ teaspoon crushed red
    pepper flakes
2 tablespoons white wine vinegar
Juice of 1 lime
½ cup extra-virgin olive oil
Sea salt and freshly ground
    black pepper

Combine the cilantro, parsley, oregano, honey, garlic, red pepper flakes, vinegar, and lime juice in a food processor or blender and purée until smooth. With the motor running, gradually add the oil. Season with salt and pepper to taste and serve or refrigerate in an airtight container until ready to serve or up to 1 week.

southwestern steak tacos with chopped charred summer vegetables

These are best when corn and tomatoes are in season, but if you want to make them at other times of the year, you can get away with using frozen corn (substitute 1 cup for the 2 ears) and good vine-ripened hothouse tomatoes, which get sweeter when they're cooked. If it's grilling season, you can cook the steak and vegetables as well as warm the tortillas on an outdoor grill instead of the stove.

SERVES 2 TO 4

. . . .

1 1-pound New York strip steak 1½ inches thick

1 lime, halved

1 teaspoon ground cumin

1 teaspoon chili powder
Freshly ground black pepper

2 ears of corn, husks and silks removed

1 red bell pepper, cored, seeded, and cut into 2-inch chunks

1 bunch of scallions, cleaned and trimmed

2 tomatoes, cored and quartered
Sea salt

4 corn tortillas, warmed (see "Warming Tortillas," page 97)

2 cups loosely packed mixed baby greens or arugula, washed and drained

½ cup Cilantro-Lime Sour Cream (recipe follows)

Place the steak on a plate and squeeze the lime juice over both sides; sprinkle both sides with the cumin, chili powder, and pepper, and rub the seasonings into the steak. Set the steak aside to rest at room temperature while you grill the vegetables.

Heat a grill pan or cast-iron skillet over medium-high heat until hot. (Or prepare a hot fire in a charcoal or gas grill.) Put the corn, bell pepper, and scallions in the skillet to grill for about 5 minutes, turning often, until the vegetables are charred in places and the scallions are wilted. Transfer the vegetables to a plate to cool slightly. Add the tomatoes to the skillet to char for about 5 minutes, turning often. Remove the tomatoes to the plate with the other vegetables.

(Recipe continues)

Try This!

Flavored sour cream is a delicious topping for soups, tacos, baked potatoes, or grilled meats. Use other spices, such as chili powder, curry, or ground coriander in place of the cumin. Substitute fresh mint, parsley, or thyme, for the cilantro, or use fresh lemon or orange juice instead of the lime juice.

Roughly chop the pepper, scallions, and tomatoes and return them to the plate. Cut the corn kernels off the cob and mix with the other vegetables. Season the vegetables with salt and pepper, cover loosely with foil to keep warm, and set aside.

Season both sides of the steak with salt and grill for 5 to 6 minutes per side. Move the steak away from the direct fire, close the grill or cover the steak with foil, and cook for another 7 to 8 minutes, until an instant-read thermometer reads 120°F for medium-rare (for medium, cook the steaks a few more minutes, until the thermometer reads 130°F). Transfer the steak to a cutting board, cover loosely with foil, and let rest for about 5 minutes. Thinly slice the steak on the diagonal against the grain.

To assemble the tacos, lay the warmed tortillas on a work surface or platter. Lay the steak slices down the center of the tortillas and spoon the vegetables over the steak, dividing them evenly. Top with the mixed greens and a dollop of the Cilantro-Lime Sour Cream, fold in half, and serve.

CILANTRO-LIME SOUR CREAM
Makes about 1 cup

1 cup sour cream
2 tablespoons chopped
    fresh cilantro
1 teaspoon ground cumin
1 teaspoon hot sauce, such as
    Texas Pete or Tabasco
Grated zest and juice of 1 lime

Combine the sour cream, cilantro, cumin, hot sauce, and lime zest and juice in a small bowl and stir to mix. Serve or refrigerate in an airtight container until ready to serve or up to 1 week.

WARMING TORTILLAS

The best way I know to warm corn or flour tortillas is how it's done in Mexico—directly over the flame of a stovetop burner or outdoor grill. (This method also works on an electric stove, though the tortillas may take slightly longer to warm.) To warm the tortillas this way, place one tortilla directly on the burner of a gas or electric stove over high heat and cook it, turning it constantly with tongs to prevent it from browning or crisping, until it's warmed through but still soft. Wrap the tortilla in a clean dishtowel or aluminum foil and repeat with the remaining tortillas. Alternatively, to warm the tortillas in the microwave, stack them, wrap them in a damp, clean dishtowel, and place them in the microwave for about 1 minute.

pan-seared tuna tacos with mango-avocado salsa

I make these often when I'm having last-minute guests. I find that dinners are always a bit more festive when people assemble their own food, as they do with these tacos; it just loosens everybody up.

SERVES 4 TO 6

Juice of 1 orange

Juice of 1 lime

1 tablespoon olive oil, plus extra for oiling the grill

2 scallions, minced (white and green parts)

½ teaspoon ground cumin

1 garlic clove, minced

1 pound ahi tuna steak, about 1 inch thick

Sea salt and freshly ground black pepper

6 to 8 7-inch flour tortillas, warmed (see "Warming Tortillas," page 97)

2 cups loosely packed arugula

1 cup shredded green cabbage

Mango-Avocado Salsa (recipe follows)

Prepare a hot fire in a charcoal or gas grill.

Stir the orange juice, lime juice, olive oil, scallions, cumin, and garlic together in a small bowl. Place the tuna in a shallow dish or large sealable plastic bag and pour half of the marinade over it, reserving the remainder for serving. Turn to coat the tuna evenly and marinate it for about 5 minutes.

Brush the grill lightly with olive oil. Remove the tuna from the marinade and discard the marinade. Season both sides of the tuna to taste with salt and pepper and grill for about 1 minute per side for medium-rare, turning only once. Transfer the tuna to a cutting board and let it rest for about 5 minutes.

Thinly slice the tuna against the grain, lay the slices on a platter, and drizzle them with the reserved marinade. Serve the tuna with the warm tortillas, arugula, cabbage, and salsa so everyone can assemble his or her own tacos.

MANGO-AVOCADO SALSA

Makes about 2 cups

½ red bell pepper, cored, seeded, and diced

2 scallions, minced (white and green parts)

1 tablespoon rice wine vinegar

1 tablespoon chopped fresh cilantro

1 garlic clove, minced

Grated zest and juice of 1 lime

½ jalapeño pepper, cored, seeded, and minced

¼ teaspoon chili powder

Sea salt and freshly ground black pepper

1 mango, halved, peeled, pitted, and cut into ½-inch cubes

1 avocado, halved, peeled, pitted, and cut into ½-inch cubes

Combine the bell pepper, scallions, vinegar, cilantro, garlic, lime zest and juice, jalapeño pepper, and chili powder together in a medium bowl. Season to taste with salt and pepper and stir to combine. Add the mango and stir again very gently. Add the avocado just before serving and toss; season with additional salt, if desired.

sara says
To cut a mango hold it upright and cut off both cheeks, being careful to avoid the pit. Cut off any flesh remaining around the pit. To peel the cheeks, halve them lengthwise, then run a knife between the peel and the flesh.

QUESADILLAS, TACOS, TOSTADAS, AND PIZZAS

cc's lobster tacos with baja fixin's

The first time my coauthor, Carolynn, came to visit Peter and me in Lake Placid, she and I picked up some cooked Maine lobsters for a last-minute dinner. I put Carolynn in charge of what to make, and she came up with lobster tacos. They were delicious.

SERVES 4

Kosher salt

2 1½-pound lobsters or 1 pound fresh cooked lobster meat

1 avocado, halved, pitted, peeled, and thinly sliced

3 limes, cut into wedges

Sea salt

8 corn tortillas, warmed (see "Warming Tortillas," page 97)

Mexican crema or sour cream thinned with buttermilk

Chipotle Salsa (recipe follows)

2 cups shredded green cabbage

Bring a large stockpot of water to a rolling boil and add salt. Put the lobsters in the water, claws first, and cook them for 12 to 14 minutes, until the tails turn bright red. Remove the lobsters from the pot and allow them to cool enough to handle. Remove the meat from the shells, pile it on a platter, and cover loosely with foil to keep warm.

Lay the avocado slices on a small plate, drizzle with the juice of one lime wedge, and sprinkle with sea salt just before serving.

To serve, scatter the remaining lime wedges around the lobster and place the platter in the center of the table with the warm tortillas, crema, Chipotle Salsa, cabbage, and avocado so guests can assemble their own tacos.

CHIPOTLE SALSA
Makes about 1 cup

¼ cup fresh cilantro leaves

3 chipotle chiles in adobo sauce

1 tomato, cored and chopped

Combine the cilantro leaves, chipotle chiles, and tomato in a blender and purée until smooth. Serve or refrigerate in an airtight container until ready to serve or up to 1 week.

italian baguette pizzas with sausage and peppers

The thin crisp exterior and light airy interior of a baguette makes a delicious thick pizza crust. You can use sweet sausage for these, but my philosophy is: Why would you eat a sweet sausage when you could eat a spicy one?

SERVES 4 TO 6

- 1 tablespoon olive oil, plus extra for brushing the bread and for drizzling
- 1 pound Italian pork sausage (spicy or sweet)
- 1 baguette (about 20 inches long), halved lengthwise
- 2 garlic cloves, smashed
- ½ cup Savory Tomato Sauce (page 121 or your favorite)

- 2 roasted red bell peppers (See "Roasting Peppers," page 79; or from a jar or deli case), cut into 1-inch pieces
- 8 ounces fresh mozzarella cheese, thinly sliced
- 2 tablespoons chopped fresh flat-leaf parsley
  Sea salt and freshly ground black pepper

Preheat the broiler.

Heat the olive oil in a large skillet or brush a grill pan lightly with the oil. Cook the sausage, turning often, for 8 to 10 minutes, until light brown and cooked through. Transfer the sausage to a cutting board to rest for about 5 minutes, then thinly slice the sausage on the diagonal.

Brush the cut side of the baguette lightly with olive oil and rub the bread liberally with the smashed garlic cloves, discarding what remains of the cloves. Place the baguette, oiled side up, under the broiler for about 1 minute, until it's lightly toasted.

Reduce the oven temperature to 400°F degrees.

Place the baguette halves, toasted side up, on a rimmed baking sheet. Spread the tomato sauce evenly on the baguette and top with the sausage slices, roasted peppers, and mozzarella, distributing the ingredients evenly. Sprinkle the pizzas with the parsley, season to taste with salt and pepper, and bake them for 13 to 15 minutes, until the cheese is light brown and bubbly. Drizzle the pizzas with olive oil, cut each baguette half into several manageable-size pieces, and serve warm.

sara says———
When toasting bread under the broiler, watch it carefully, as it can burn very quickly.

QUESADILLAS, TACOS, TOSTADAS, AND PIZZAS

pizza variations

The notion that pizza has to be topped with Italian ingredients went out the door with the invention of ham and pineapple pizza. I make pizzas with all kinds of ingredients—most often leftovers. Especially if you're cooking for one or two people, a small chunk of cheese or a few slices of leftover chicken or steak are all you need. Below are some of my most successful combinations. You can use them to make pizzas on any type of crust: pita bread, baguette, English muffins, or store-bought dough; or use them to make a tart using puff pastry.

GRILLED CHICKEN CAESAR PIZZA

Brush the crusts of your choice lightly with your favorite Caesar or tangy Italian dressing. Top with thinly sliced grilled chicken, a few large hearts of romaine leaves, and a sprinkling of freshly ground black pepper and grated Parmesan cheese. Bake the pizzas and sprinkle with chopped fresh parsley before serving.

SAUSAGE, SQUASH, AND GOAT CHEESE PIZZA

Brush the crusts of your choice liberally with olive oil. Top with crumbled cooked pork or lamb sausage, sliced tomatoes, roasted red pepper strips, grilled summer squash, and crumbled goat cheese. Bake the pizzas and sprinkle them with chopped fresh oregano before serving.

VEGETARIAN EVERYTHING PIZZA

Spread a thin layer of tomato sauce evenly over the crusts of your choice. Scatter chopped pepperoncini peppers, marinated artichokes, mushrooms, eggplant, sun-dried tomatoes, capers, olives, and roasted cipollini onions over the pizzas. Top with a layer of grated Parmesan, pecorino, smoked mozzarella, or fontina cheese, and bake.

SPICY SOUTHWESTERN CHICKEN AND CORN PIZZA

Spread a thin layer of basil pesto evenly over the crusts of your choice. Top with thinly sliced grilled chicken, a handful of corn kernels, roasted red pepper strips, minced jalapeño pepper, shredded Monterey Jack or pepper Jack cheese, and several thin slices of fresh mozzarella cheese. Bake the pizzas and sprinkle with fresh flat-leaf parsley and freshly ground black pepper before serving.

CARAMELIZED ONIONS, BACON, MUSHROOMS, AND GOAT CHEESE PIZZA

Thinly slice a red onion and cook in butter and olive oil over low heat for

30 to 35 minutes, until soft and caramelized. Spread the onion evenly over the crusts of your choice. Top with a few halved roasted garlic cloves, cooked bacon cut into bite-size pieces, and crumbled goat cheese. Bake the pizzas and sprinkle with chopped fresh rosemary before serving.

BARBECUED CHICKEN, BACON, AND CILANTRO PIZZA

Spread a thin layer of barbecue sauce over the crusts of your choice. Scatter shredded grilled or barbecued chicken over the pizzas and top with caramelized onions, crumbled crisp bacon, and shredded fresh or smoked mozzarella cheese. Bake the pizzas and sprinkle with fresh cilantro leaves before serving.

GRILLED EGGPLANT, TOMATOES, AND ROASTED GARLIC PIZZA

Spread a thin layer of prepared basil pesto evenly over the crusts of your choice. Top with halved roasted garlic cloves, grilled eggplant slices, grilled plum tomatoes (or sun-dried tomatoes), and sliced fresh mozzarella cheese. Bake the pizzas and sprinkle with thinly sliced fresh basil leaves and freshly ground black pepper before serving.

GREEK PIZZA *(Pictured on page 84)*

Spread a thin layer of pesto over the crust of your choice. Top with a mixture of arugula, chopped olives, red onion, chopped mint, and oil and red wine vinegar. Bake the pizza and sprinkle with fresh oregano before serving.

FRESH MOZZARELLA CHEESE, ROASTED RED PEPPERS, TOMATOES, AND PESTO PIZZA

Spread a thin layer of prepared basil pesto evenly over the crusts of your choice and top with grilled tomatoes (or sun-dried tomatoes), roasted red peppers strips, and slices of fresh mozzarella cheese. Bake the pizzas and sprinkle with fresh thinly sliced basil leaves before serving.

FOUR-CHEESE PIZZA

Spread a thin layer of prepared basil pesto or tomato sauce evenly over the crusts of your choice and top with grated mozzarella cheese, fontina cheese, feta cheese, and Parmesan cheese (or for a smoky version, smoked mozzarella cheese, goat cheese, and Cheddar cheese). Bake the pizzas and sprinkle with fresh herbs (chopped parsley or oregano or thinly sliced fresh basil leaves) and freshly ground black pepper before serving.

mom's pepperoni english muffin pizzas

Every American mother probably made some version of English muffin pizzas for her children, and they're all probably pretty similar to those my mom made for my sister Judy and me. The pizzas always felt like a special treat and I still love them. You could use fresh mozzarella, but to be truly authentic, you'd use the "low moisture" mozzarella from the dairy case, the stuff we all grew up with.

SERVES 4

. . . .

- 4 English muffins, split
- 1 cup Savory Tomato Sauce (page 121; or your favorite)
- 2 tablespoons chopped fresh herbs (such as basil, parsley, or oregano, or a combination)

- 2 ounces pepperoni, thinly sliced
- 4 ounces mozzarella cheese, shredded (about 1 cup)
- 2 tablespoons chopped fresh oregano

Preheat the broiler.

Toast the English muffins in the broiler or toaster until they're golden brown and crisp.

Place the muffins cut side up on a rimmed baking sheet. Stir the mixed herbs into the tomato sauce and spread 2 tablespoons of the sauce over each English muffin half. Top the pizzas with the pepperoni, dividing it evenly, sprinkle each with about 2 tablespoons of the mozzarella, and sprinkle with the oregano. Place the pizzas under the broiler for about 2 minutes, until the cheese melts and the pepperoni is sizzling. Serve warm.

heirloom tomato tarts with goat cheese and fresh rosemary

I always keep puff pastry in the freezer. It makes a buttery and delicious tart crust and (the best part) it's so convenient to use. I serve these tarts with a green salad and call it a meal. This recipe makes two tarts, so you can give one tart to a friend or keep it around for snacking.

EACH TART SERVES 4; MAKES TWO 4- x 12-INCH TARTS

- 1 sheet frozen puff pastry (such as Pepperidge Farm or Dufour's), thawed in the refrigerator
- 1 large egg, lightly beaten
- 1 tablespoon milk
- 4 ounces fresh goat cheese, crumbled (about 1 cup)
- 2 tablespoons fresh rosemary or thyme
- 4 heirloom tomatoes or other good tomatoes, cored and thinly sliced
- 2 tablespoons olive oil
  Sea salt and freshly ground black pepper

Cut the sheet of puff pastry in half lengthwise and cut a ¼-inch-wide strip from each edge of each sheet, reserving the strips. Place the pastry on a baking sheet.

Whisk the egg and milk together to make an egg wash. Brush the edges of the two sheets with the egg wash. Place the cut pastry strips along the edges of each of the large sheets to form a raised border and press the strips gently to adhere.

Stir the goat cheese and half of the rosemary together in a small bowl until the cheese is soft and creamy. Spread the cheese in an even layer on the bottom of each tart and arrange the tomato slices over the cheese. Brush the tomatoes with the olive oil, sprinkle with the remaining rosemary, and season with salt and pepper. Brush the pastry edges with the remaining egg wash and place the tarts in the refrigerator to chill for about 30 minutes.

Preheat the oven to 400°F.

Bake the tarts for 18 to 20 minutes, until the pastry is golden brown and puffed up. Cut each tart into four equal portions and serve warm.

sara says

Once you've taken the puff pastry out of the refrigerator, you need to work quickly; it becomes too sticky to work with once it's warm. Also, the pastry comes out flakier if it goes in the oven cold.

A pizza cutter makes cutting the puff pastry really easy.

pasta and noodles

EVEN WHEN IT LOOKS LIKE there's nothing in the house to eat, you can probably dig up some pasta. Tossed with a handful of fresh, flavorful ingredients, pasta makes a really satisfying one-bowl meal. Many of these recipes take advantage of pantry staples and ingredients that are easy to have on hand: canned tomatoes, canned beans, sausage, and cheese. Others are based on flavorful ingredients, like heirloom tomatoes and fresh herbs, so you can create vibrant dishes with just a few ingredients. Although they may seem exotic, Asian noodles, like soba, udon, and rice noodles, are just as easy to prepare as conventional pasta. And to ensure that a hearty, delicious meal is never more than a half a pound of pasta away, I also included a list of Nine Quick and Easy Pasta Sauces with the idea that you're bound to have the ingredients to make at least *one* of them.

summer spaghetti with heirloom tomatoes, crumbled feta cheese, and fresh basil

During tomato season, we use heirloom tomatoes wherever we can at the Market. Customers just can't get enough of them and neither can the cooks. During that time, we offer this pasta every day, at room temperature. If you can't find heirloom tomatoes, any good, sweet, summer tomatoes will do, but if it's not summertime and you don't have really good tomatoes, this isn't the recipe to make.

See photograph on page 111.

SERVES 4 TO 6

. . . .

Kosher salt	3 tablespoons chopped fresh flat-leaf parsley
8 ounces spaghetti	2 tablespoons capers, drained
2 tablespoons olive oil, plus more for tossing the pasta	2 tablespoons red wine vinegar
3 garlic cloves, minced	15 basil leaves, thinly sliced
½ teaspoon crushed red pepper flakes	Sea salt and freshly ground black pepper to taste
1 pound heirloom tomatoes, cored and diced	4 ounces feta cheese, crumbled (about 1 cup)

Bring a large pot of water to a boil and add salt. Stir in the spaghetti and cook until al dente, 8 to 9 minutes, or according to the package instructions. Reserve a cupful of the pasta cooking water, then drain the spaghetti, drizzle lightly with olive oil, and toss to coat. Set aside.

Meanwhile, heat the 2 tablespoons of olive oil in a large skillet over medium heat. Add the garlic and red pepper flakes and sauté for about 1 minute, stirring constantly so the garlic doesn't brown. Add the spaghetti, tomatoes, parsley, capers, vinegar, and basil, and season to taste with salt and pepper. Place the skillet over medium-high heat, add enough of the reserved pasta water to make the pasta slippery, and cook for about 2 minutes, tossing the spaghetti to combine all the ingredients, until warmed through. Serve warm or at room temperature, topped with the crumbled feta cheese.

sara says
Always reserve a cupful of the water the pasta was cooked in. If the sauce is too thick or sticky, a little added pasta water will loosen it just enough to coat the pasta nicely.

PASTA AND NOODLES

linguine with spicy chorizo and goat cheese

I make this using Spanish chorizo, which is a hard, smoked sausage that can be sliced. The Mexican variety is soft and needs to be cooked before you eat it. If you can't find Spanish chorizo, use Mexican chorizo or spicy Italian pork sausage in its place, but remove the casings and crumble the sausage instead of slicing it, and be sure to cook it all the way through.

SERVES 4 TO 6

. . . .

2 tablespoons olive oil

2 links Spanish chorizo (about 8 ounces), thinly sliced on the diagonal

1 red onion, chopped
Kosher salt

8 ounces linguine

4 cups loosely packed spinach, washed, drained, and trimmed of tough stems

2 tomatoes, cored and chopped

¼ cup dry red wine

4 ounces goat cheese, crumbled (about 1 cup)

¼ cup chopped fresh flat-leaf parsley

2 tablespoons chopped fresh oregano or marjoram

6 fresh basil leaves, thinly sliced
Sea salt and freshly ground black pepper

Heat the olive oil in a large nonstick skillet over medium-high heat. Add the chorizo and onion and cook and stir for 3 to 4 minutes, until the sausage is brown and warmed through and the onion is tender and translucent. (If you're using Mexican chorizo or Italian sausage, continue to cook it until the sausage is done.)

Meanwhile, bring a large pot of water to a boil and add salt. Stir in the linguine and cook until al dente, 8 to 9 minutes, or according to the package instructions.

Reserve a cupful of the pasta cooking water, drain the linguine, and transfer it to the skillet with the sausage and onion. Place the skillet over medium-high heat; add the spinach, tomatoes, wine, and enough of the reserved pasta water to make the pasta slippery. Cook and stir for 1 or 2 minutes, until the spinach is wilted and the ingredients are warmed through. Remove from the heat and stir in the goat cheese, parsley, oregano, and basil. Season to taste with salt and pepper and serve warm.

sara says
Unless you're making a cold pasta salad, don't rinse pasta after cooking it. The starch on the pasta helps thicken the sauce.

springtime capellini with fresh ricotta cheese and mixed herbs

Because of all the fresh herbs and the delicate taste of ricotta, I think of this as a springtime dish although I make it almost year-round. You can get fresh ricotta at cheese shops and Italian import stores, but if you can't find it, the supermarket stuff works fine; just use the whole-milk, not skim, variety.

SERVES 4 TO 6

Kosher salt

8 ounces capellini

¼ cup olive oil, plus extra for tossing the pasta

2 scallions, minced (white and green parts)

2 garlic cloves, minced

4 cups loosely packed mixed baby greens

½ cup fresh flat-leaf parsley leaves, finely chopped

¼ cup snipped fresh chives

¼ cup fresh dill

10 fresh basil leaves, torn into small pieces

Grated zest and juice of 1 lemon

Sea salt and freshly ground black pepper

½ cup freshly grated Parmesan cheese

½ cup fresh whole-milk ricotta cheese (about 4 ounces)

Try This!

To make this light pasta into a more substantial one-dish meal, top it with garlic-sautéed shrimp or slices of grilled chicken and strips of roasted red peppers.

Bring a large pot water to a boil and add salt. Stir in the capellini and cook until al dente, about 2 minutes or according to the package instructions. Reserve a cupful of the pasta cooking water, drain the capellini, drizzle it lightly with olive oil, and toss to coat. Set aside.

Meanwhile, heat the ¼ cup of olive oil in a large skillet over medium heat. Add the scallions and cook and stir for about 1 minute. Add the garlic and cook for 1 minute, stirring constantly so it doesn't brown. Reduce the heat to low and add the capellini, greens, parsley, chives, dill, basil, and lemon zest and juice, and season to taste with salt and pepper. Sprinkle with half of the Parmesan cheese, spoon the ricotta cheese into the pan, and toss gently to mix. Add enough of the reserved pasta water to make the pasta slippery and cook until the ingredients are warmed through. Sprinkle the pasta with the remaining Parmesan cheese and serve warm.

rigatoni with sausage, cannellini bean, and swiss chard ragù

Because it's so big and toothsome, rigatoni seems to demand a hearty, wintry sauce like this one. It's just the kind of comforting one-dish meal you want on a cold night.

SERVES 4 TO 6

- 1 tablespoon olive oil
- 1 onion, diced
- 3 garlic cloves, minced
- 1½ pounds Italian sausage (spicy or sweet), casings removed
- 1 28-ounce can of chopped tomatoes (with their juices)
- 2 cups chicken broth
  Kosher salt
- 8 ounces rigatoni
- 1 bunch of Swiss chard, washed, drained, and roughly chopped
- 12 fresh basil leaves, thinly sliced
- 1 tablespoon chopped fresh oregano
- 1 15-ounce can cannellini beans or navy beans (about 2 cups), rinsed and drained
  Sea salt and freshly ground black pepper
- ⅓ cup freshly grated Parmesan cheese, plus extra for passing at the table

Heat the olive oil in a large skillet over medium heat. Add the onion and cook and stir for 3 to 4 minutes, until tender and translucent. Add the garlic and sauté for 1 minute without browning. Add the sausage and break it up into small pieces. Cook and stir the sausage for about 5 minutes, until it's light brown. Drain the grease from the pan. Add the tomatoes with their juice and the chicken broth. Reduce the heat to low, and simmer the sauce for about 30 minutes, stirring occasionally.

Meanwhile, bring a large pot of water to a boil and add salt. Stir in the rigatoni and cook until al dente, 7 to 8 minutes, or according to the package instructions.

Reserve a cupful of the pasta cooking water, then drain the pasta and add it to the skillet with the tomato sauce. Add the chard, basil, oregano, beans, and enough of the reserved water to make the pasta slippery. Cook for 3 to 4 minutes, until the beans are warmed through and the chard is wilted. Season the pasta with salt and pepper, if desired, and serve warm, with the Parmesan cheese sprinkled on top and more to pass at the table.

*sara says*_____
To prevent the dreaded fate of overcooked pasta, start checking for doneness a few minutes before the time indicated on the package.

nine quick and easy pasta sauces

Each of the sauces that follow will be enough for 8 ounces of warm, freshly cooked pasta; always reserve a bit of the cooking water to toss with the sauce and hot pasta.

Carbonara Sauce

Fry 2 or 3 slices of bacon in a large skillet until crisp. Transfer the bacon to a paper towel–lined plate to drain and pour the grease from the skillet. Whisk 1 large egg in a bowl with ½ cup heavy cream, sea salt, and freshly ground black pepper. Put 8 ounces of warm just-cooked pasta into the skillet you cooked the bacon in over low heat. Turn off the heat, add the egg-cream mixture and some of the hot pasta cooking water, crumble in the bacon, and toss to coat. Top with freshly grated Parmesan cheese.

GOOD WITH: spaghetti, linguine, or fettuccine.

Pepperonata Sauce

Heat 2 tablespoons of olive oil in a large skillet over medium heat and add 4 chopped red, green, or yellow bell peppers, 1 chopped red onion, and salt and black pepper. Cook and stir for about 25 minutes. Add 2 minced garlic cloves, 3 tablespoons balsamic vinegar, and ¼ cup red wine and cook the sauce for about 3 minutes longer. Remove from the heat and add 6 thinly sliced basil leaves.

GOOD WITH: penne, rigatoni, farfalle, or orecchiette.

Lemon, Garlic, and Olive Oil Sauce

Heat ¼ cup olive oil in a large skillet over medium heat, add 4 minced garlic cloves, and cook and stir for about 1 minute. Add the grated zest and juice of 2 lemons and 2 tablespoons chopped parsley and cook and stir for 1 minute more. Season with sea salt and freshly ground black pepper. Stir in ¼ cup freshly grated Parmesan cheese or ½ cup fresh ricotta cheese.

GOOD WITH: capellini, vermicelli, spaghetti, or orzo.

Wild Mushroom Sauce

Heat 3 tablespoons unsalted butter and 1 tablespoon olive oil in a large skillet over medium-high heat. Add 8 ounces cleaned wild mushrooms (such as chanterelle, porcini, yellow foot, or hedgehog), 2 minced shallots, and salt and pepper to taste; sauté, stirring constantly, for about 3 minutes, until the mushrooms are golden. Remove the mushrooms from the pan. Add ¼ cup white wine to the pan and cook it for about 1 minute to reduce slightly. Add ½ cup heavy cream, season with sea salt and freshly ground black pepper, and cook about 2 minutes, then return the mushrooms to the sauce.

GOOD WITH: conchiglie, gemelli, farfalle, or orecchiette.

Basil Pesto

Place 3 handfuls fresh basil, $\frac{1}{2}$ cup freshly grated Parmesan cheese, 2 tablespoons toasted pine nuts, 4 smashed garlic cloves, the juice of half a lemon, and sea salt and freshly ground black pepper in a blender or food processor and pulse to chop. With the motor running, add enough olive oil to make a smooth, loose paste.

GOOD WITH: orzo, orecchiette, ravioli, fusilli, conchiglie, or gemelli.

Savory Tomato Sauce

Heat 1 tablespoon olive oil in a large skillet over medium heat. Add 2 minced shallots and sauté for about 2 minutes to soften them. Add 1 minced garlic clove and a pinch of crushed red pepper flakes, and sauté for 1 minute, stirring constantly so the garlic doesn't brown. Add $\frac{1}{2}$ cup dry red wine, $1\frac{1}{2}$ pounds cored and chopped plum tomatoes or 1 28-ounce can chopped tomatoes (with their juices), 2 tablespoons chopped fresh marjoram or oregano; season with salt and pepper. Simmer for about 15 minutes to thicken.

VARIATION: Stir in $\frac{1}{4}$ cup heavy cream for Creamy Tomato Sauce

VARIATION: Add $\frac{1}{4}$ cup pitted chopped olives, 2 tablespoons drained capers, and a few chopped anchovies (if desired) for Puttanesca Sauce.

GOOD WITH: ziti, conchiglie, farfalle, or gemelli.

Sage Brown Butter Sauce *(see photo, page 112)*

Melt $\frac{1}{2}$ stick of butter over medium heat. Add 3 tablespoons of chopped sage and 10 whole sage leaves, and cook 3 minutes, swirling the pan occasionally, until the butter is brown and nutty smelling. Season the butter with salt and pepper to taste and toss with warm ravioli. Sprinkle with grated Parmesan.

GOOD WITH: pumpkin, spinach, or sweet potato ravioli.

Alfredo Sauce

Add 4 tablespoons ($\frac{1}{2}$ stick) cubed, unsalted butter, $\frac{1}{4}$ cup heavy cream, and $\frac{1}{4}$ cup freshly grated Parmesan cheese to 8 ounces of warm, just-cooked pasta in a large skillet over low heat. Toss to melt the butter and cheese and season with sea salt and freshly ground black pepper and freshly grated nutmeg, if desired.

GOOD WITH: fettuccine or linguine.

Roasted Red Pepper Sauce

Purée 2 roasted red peppers in a blender or food processor with 2 garlic cloves, 8 fresh basil leaves, and $\frac{1}{2}$ cup crumbled goat cheese. Season with sea salt and freshly ground black pepper.

GOOD WITH: ziti, rigatoni, fusilli, or conchiglie.

coconut fish stew with soba noodles and kale

A lot of kale fans like it for its rich mineral and vitamin content, but I like the way it tastes and its sturdy texture. It's ideal in a stew like this, because the hardy, slightly bitter leaves keep their character in the rich sweet broth. There are many different varieties of kale, any of which will work here, as will spinach.

SERVES 4

1 lemongrass stalk

3 garlic cloves, smashed

3 tablespoons minced peeled fresh ginger (from a 3-inch piece)

1 tablespoon chopped cilantro root

1 tablespoon honey
Juice of 1 lime

1 small fresh red or green chile, minced

1 teaspoon ground cumin

2 tablespoons peanut oil

4 6-ounce white fish fillets (such as grouper, snapper, bass, cod, or halibut, skinned), rinsed and patted dry

Sea salt and freshly ground black pepper
Kosher salt

8 ounces soba noodles or udon noodles

3 cups chicken broth

¾ cup unsweetened coconut milk

3 tablespoons Asian fish sauce

1 tablespoon light brown sugar

1 bunch of kale, trimmed of stems and roughly chopped (about 4 cups) or spinach

¼ cup fresh cilantro leaves

Remove the tough outer leaves from the lemongrass stalk. Smash the stalk with the flat side of a knife and chop it roughly. Combine half of the lemongrass, the garlic, half of the ginger, the cilantro root, honey, lime juice, half of the chile, the cumin, and 1 tablespoon of the peanut oil in a blender and purée until smooth.

Heat the remaining tablespoon of peanut oil in a large skillet over high heat. Season the fish fillets on both sides with salt and pepper and place them flesh side down in the skillet to cook for about 2 minutes, until the flesh side is golden brown. Remove the fish from the skillet and cover it with foil to keep warm.

Meanwhile, bring a large pot of water to a boil and add salt. Stir in the soba noodles and cook until al dente, 3 to 4 minutes, or according to the package instructions. Drain the noodles and divide them among four large soup plates or bowls.

Add the remaining lemongrass, ginger, and chile to the skillet you cooked the fish in and sauté for about 2 minutes, until the ingredients are fragrant. Stir in the chicken broth, coconut milk, fish sauce, and brown sugar; bring the soup to a low boil, reduce the heat, and simmer the stew for about 5 minutes to meld the flavors. Stir in the blended paste and season to taste with salt and pepper. Add the fish and kale and simmer the stew for about 2 minutes, until the fish is cooked through but still holds its shape. Turn off the heat and stir in the cilantro leaves.

To serve, carefully remove the fish fillets from the broth, place one fillet on top of each serving of noodles, and ladle the broth and kale over the fish.

sara says_____
Don't let the soup come to a boil after you add the fish or the fish will be tough.

❧
Try This!
For a more Caribbean-inflected stew, serve this over a mound of Lemon-Coconut Basmati Rice Pilaf (page 221) or try using udon noodles.

rice noodles with hoisin-marinated pork and wilted spinach

At the Market, anything with hoisin sauce is well received by our customers, and this dish is no exception.

SERVES 4

Bean thread noodles (also called cellophane noodles), which are made with mung bean flour, can be used inter-changeably with rice noodles. In either case, I use linguine-shaped noodles. Use what you like, but note that the soaking time will vary depending on the thickness of the noodles you use.

- 1 1-pound pork tenderloin
- 2 tablespoons hoisin sauce
- 1 tablespoon light soy sauce or tamari
- 1 tablespoon Thai chili paste
- 6 ounces rice noodles
- 1 tablespoon canola oil
  Sea salt and freshly ground black pepper
- 3 scallions, minced (white and green parts)
- 2 garlic cloves, minced
- 1 1-inch piece of fresh ginger, peeled and thinly sliced
- 1 small fresh red or green chile, thinly sliced
- ¼ cup mirin or Chinese cooking wine
- 2 tablespoons Asian fish sauce
- 1 tablespoon rice wine vinegar
- 1 teaspoon sugar
- 6 cups loosely packed spinach
- ¼ cup fresh cilantro leaves

Trim the pork tenderloin of sinew and fat, rinse, and pat dry. Place the tenderloin in a shallow glass bowl or in a large sealable plastic bag.

Stir the hoisin sauce, soy sauce, and chili paste together in a small bowl, pour the marinade over the tenderloin, and turn the pork or shake the bag to coat the pork. Cover the bowl or close the bag and marinate the pork for about 30 minutes at room temperature or up to overnight in the refrigerator.

Bring a medium pot of water to a boil. Remove the pot from the heat and immerse the noodles in the water. Let the noodles stand in the hot water, stirring occasionally, for 5 to 6 minutes or until just tender. Drain the noodles and set aside.

Heat the oil in a large skillet over medium-high heat. Remove the pork from the marinade, season all sides with salt and pepper, and place it in the skillet to sear for 8 minutes, turning every 2 minutes to brown all four sides. Reduce the heat to low and cook the pork for about 3 minutes, turning occasionally. Add the scallions, garlic, ginger, and chile, and

cook and stir for about 1 minute. Remove the skillet from the heat and transfer the pork to a cutting board to rest, loosely covered with foil, for about 5 minutes, leaving the vegetables in the skillet.

Stir the mirin, fish sauce, vinegar, and sugar together in a small bowl and add it to the skillet. Add the noodles and spinach, toss gently to combine, and cook over medium heat for about 2 minutes, until the noodles are heated through and the spinach is wilted. Remove from the heat, stir in the cilantro, and season to taste with salt and pepper.

Thinly slice the tenderloin and arrange on the noodles. Serve warm.

Individual Prosciutto, Spinach, and Egg "Pies"

Soft-Boiled Eggs with Herbed Toast Fingers

Wild Mushroom Toasts with Poached Eggs

Grilled Bacon, Egg, and Cheddar Cheese Breakfast Sandwiches

Breakfast Tostadas with Fried Eggs and Guacamole

Ricotta Cheese Tartlets with Spinach and Sautéed Sweet Onions

Leftover Steak and Fried Egg Tostadas with Chipotle Salsa

Chilaquiles and Andouille Sausage Scramble with Salsa Verde

Smoked Salmon Toasts with Poached Eggs and Dijon-Dill Sauce

anytime eggs

WHEN IT COMES TO CONVENIENCE FOOD, you can't do much better than eggs: they're nourishing, they cook in minutes, and they'll keep in your refrigerator for weeks. Eggs seem to invite the addition of just about anything savory—herbs, cheese, vegetables, meats, and fish—so when you're making a meal out of eggs, the possibilities are endless. The only challenge—for some people—is to get over the idea that eggs are just for breakfast. In these recipes, I take you beyond bacon and eggs to poached eggs served atop grilled wild mushrooms, eggs scrambled with crisp tortillas and andouille sausage, or eggs baked into elegant individual pies with a prosciutto "crust." The tried-and-true combination does make an appearance in the form of Grilled Bacon, Egg, and Cheddar Cheese Breakfast Sandwiches (page 133), which, trust me, are as good a way to end a day as they are to begin it.

individual prosciutto, spinach, and egg "pies"

We make these elegant little pies often at the Market. There's no crust involved; the prosciutto forms the outside of the pie. Customers love to get them when they're on the run because they're easy to eat out of hand. For the same reason, they're great for a weekend brunch or picnic.

SERVES 4 TO 6

. . . .

Olive oil for greasing the muffin tins

6 thin slices prosciutto

6 large eggs

1 cup loosely packed spinach, roughly chopped

1 ounce Cheddar cheese, shredded (about ¼ cup)

12 grape tomatoes or small cherry tomatoes, halved

Sea salt and freshly ground black pepper

Preheat the oven to 350°F. Lightly grease a 6-cup muffin tin with olive oil.

Line the muffin cups with the prosciutto slices, pressing the prosciutto into the bottom and sides of each cup. (The prosciutto slices will overlap each other on top of the tin.) Crack 1 egg into each cup. Sprinkle the spinach over the eggs, then the Cheddar cheese, dividing them evenly. Top each serving with 4 tomato halves and season with salt and pepper. Bake the pies for 15 to 18 minutes, until the egg whites are firm and the yolks are starting to set but are still soft in the center. Set them aside to cool for about 5 minutes.

Run a knife around the edges of each cup to loosen, then lift the pies out of the tin. Serve warm or at room temperature.

*sara says*_____
You can double this recipe to fill an entire 12-cup muffin tin. Extra pies are delicious the next day, and they also make a nice treat to take to a neighbor.

soft-boiled eggs with herbed toast fingers

Soft-boiled eggs are sort of a forgotten food—and they shouldn't be. They're so healthy and light, and they require you to eat with your hands, which I know many people like to do. I cut the bread into little fingers because they're easier to dip into the egg that way, and I dress it up with fresh herbs.

SERVES 4

4 thick slices whole-grain bread, each cut into 4 rectangles

2 tablespoons olive oil

1 tablespoon chopped fresh dill

1 tablespoon chopped fresh parsley

Sea salt and freshly ground black pepper to taste

4 large eggs

Preheat the oven to 400°F.

Place the bread slices on a rimmed baking sheet and brush them lightly on one side with the olive oil. Sprinkle with the dill and parsley, season to taste with salt and pepper, and bake for 12 to 15 minutes, until golden brown and crisp.

Meanwhile, place the eggs in a saucepan large enough to hold them in a single layer. Fill the pan with enough cold water to cover the eggs by several inches and bring to a boil over high heat, watching closely so the eggs don't boil for more than a few seconds. Remove the pan from the heat, cover, and let it sit for about 2 minutes. (If you prefer medium-boiled eggs, let them sit about 3 minutes, or 8 minutes for hard-boiled eggs.)

To serve, place each egg in an eggcup or small bowl and cut off and discard the top third of the eggshell. Season the inside of the egg with salt and pepper and serve each egg with four of the toast fingers for dipping.

wild mushroom toasts with poached eggs

We always have some variation on poached eggs on toast at the Market. Poaching lets the pure, delicate flavor of the eggs shine through without any distraction, as with these wild mushrooms.

See photograph on page 127.

SERVES 4

. . . .

2 tablespoons unsalted butter

1 tablespoon olive oil, plus more for brushing the bread

4 ounces wild mushrooms, trimmed and sliced if needed

1 shallot, minced

Sea salt and freshly ground black pepper

1 tablespoon chopped fresh chives, plus more for garnish

4 1-inch-thick slices crusty, rustic-style bread

1 teaspoon white vinegar

4 large eggs

sara says_____
Use whatever wild mush-rooms you like or that are available to you (such as lobster, chanterelle, blue foot, oyster, or porcini).

Preheat the broiler.

Heat the butter with the olive oil in a large skillet over medium-high heat until hot. Add the mushrooms and shallot and sauté for 2 to 3 minutes, stirring often, until golden brown and soft; season with salt and pepper to taste and stir in the chives. Remove the mushrooms from the heat, and keep warm.

Brush one side of the bread slices lightly with olive oil. Place under the broiler for about 1 minute per side to toast lightly.

To poach the eggs, fill a deep skillet half-full with water. Add the vinegar, bring to a low boil over high heat, and reduce the heat so the water simmers. Break one egg into a small dish and carefully slide the egg into the simmering water. Repeat with the remaining eggs and poach them for about 2 minutes, spooning the poaching water over the tops of the eggs while they cook, until the egg whites are firm and the yolks are just starting to set but are still soft in the center.

Remove the eggs with a slotted spoon, dab them on a paper towel to drain the excess water, then place one egg on each toast. Top the eggs with the mushrooms and chives. Season with additional salt and pepper if desired, and serve warm.

grilled bacon, egg, and cheddar cheese breakfast sandwiches

In the summertime, when we're in Lake Placid with a house full of guests, the skillet stays on the stove for several hours each morning while Peter makes these to order as guests get up.

SERVES 4

8 thick slices nitrate-free bacon

1 tablespoon olive oil

1 tablespoon unsalted butter, plus extra for buttering the bread

4 large eggs

Sea salt and freshly ground black pepper

8 slices whole-grain bread

4 slices Cheddar cheese

Heat a large skillet over medium heat. Add the bacon and cook, turning several times, until crisp. Drain on paper towels.

Heat half of the olive oil with half of the butter in a large nonstick skillet over medium heat until hot. Crack 2 of the eggs into the skillet and fry them for about 1 minute per side for over-easy, longer if you like them more well done. Season the eggs to taste with salt and pepper, transfer them to a plate, and cover them loosely with foil to keep warm. Repeat, heating the remaining butter and oil and frying the remaining 2 eggs in the same way.

Spread one side of each slice of bread liberally with butter and place 2 of the slices buttered side down in the skillet over medium-high heat. Put 1 fried egg, 2 slices of bacon, and 1 slice of cheese on top of each piece of bread and top with 2 of the remaining bread slices, buttered side up. Grill the sandwiches for about 2 minutes, until the bread is golden brown. Carefully flip the sandwiches and grill on the other side for about 2 minutes, until the bread is golden brown and the cheese is melted.

Transfer the sandwiches to a cutting board and cover them loosely with foil to keep warm. Repeat the process, cooking the remaining two sandwiches in the same way. Slice the sandwiches in half and serve warm.

breakfast tostadas with fried eggs and guacamole

I order huevos rancheros whenever I see them on a menu. When I make them at home, I use fresh salsa in place of stewed tomato sauce and grill rather than fry the tortillas to make a lighter dish. I cook the eggs over-easy so the yolks spill out onto the plate, softening the tortillas and creating a kind of sauce. Cook the eggs to your liking.

SERVES 2 TO 4

4   corn tortillas
1   tablespoon olive oil, plus extra
    for brushing the tortillas
1   tablespoon unsalted butter
4   large eggs
1   cup prepared black bean dip
    Sea salt and freshly ground
    black pepper

1   cup Salsa Fresca (page 90)
2   ounces goat cheese, crumbled
    (about ½ cup)
    Guacamole (recipe follows)
2   scallions, thinly sliced (white
    and green parts)

Brush both sides of the tortillas lightly with olive oil. Heat a grill pan or cast-iron skillet over high heat and place one tortilla in the skillet to grill for about 2 minutes per side, until light brown and crisp. Wrap the tortilla in a clean dishcloth and repeat, cooking the remaining tortillas in the same way.

To fry the eggs, melt half of the butter with half of the olive oil in a large nonstick skillet over medium-high heat and heat until hot. Crack 2 of the eggs into the skillet and fry them for about 1 minute per side for over-easy, longer if you like your eggs more well done. Remove the eggs to a plate and cover them loosely with foil to keep warm. Repeat, heating the remaining butter and oil and frying the remaining eggs in the same way.

To assemble the tostadas, spread each tortilla with ¼ cup of the bean dip, place a fried egg on top, and season to taste with salt and pepper. Spoon 2 tablespoons of salsa over each egg, sprinkle with the crumbled goat cheese, dollop a spoonful of guacamole, sprinkle with the scallions, and serve warm, with the remaining salsa and guacamole on the side.

Quick Fix
You can use a can of refried beans in place of the bean dip, and jarred salsa instead of homemade.

GUACAMOLE
Makes about 1 cup

1 avocado, halved, pitted, and peeled
3 scallions, minced (white and
   green parts)
1½ tablespoons chopped fresh
   cilantro
1 jalapeño pepper, cored, seeded,
   and minced
Juice of half a lime
Sea salt and freshly ground
   black pepper

Mash the avocado in a small bowl
with the scallions, cilantro, and
jalapeño pepper. Stir in the lime juice,
season to taste with salt and pepper,
and serve immediately.

ricotta cheese tartlets with greens and sautéed sweet onions

There's something about tarts that feels special. These are so easy to throw together and they bake in less than 20 minutes. Use tart pans with removable bottoms to make removing the tarts a breeze. If you don't have 4-inch tart pans, you can make this recipe using a large (9-inch) tart pan and cut the tart into quarters to serve. Note that the cooking time will be longer for the large tart.

SERVES 4

1 tablespoon olive oil, plus extra for greasing the tart pans
  Dried bread crumbs for dusting the tart pans
2 cups fresh ricotta cheese (about 1 pound)
½ cup freshly grated Parmesan cheese
2 large eggs, lightly beaten

  Sea salt and freshly ground black pepper
1 red onion, thinly sliced
1 tablespoon balsamic vinegar
1 tablespoon sugar
1 teaspoon chopped fresh rosemary
2 cups loosely packed spinach or arugula, washed and drained, stems trimmed

Preheat the oven to 350°F. Lightly grease four 4-inch tart pans with olive oil; dust with bread crumbs and shake off any excess crumbs. Place the prepared tart pans on a rimmed baking sheet and set aside.

Stir the ricotta cheese, Parmesan cheese, and eggs in a large bowl and season with salt and pepper. Spoon the cheese mixture into the tart pans, dividing it evenly, and bake the tarts for 18 to 20 minutes, until they puff up slightly and the tops are golden brown. Remove the tarts from the oven and let them cool slightly before removing them from the pans.

Meanwhile, heat the tablespoon of olive oil in a large skillet over medium-high heat. Add the onion, reduce the heat to medium, and sauté for 3 to 4 minutes, until tender and translucent. Stir in the vinegar, sugar, and rosemary. Reduce the heat to low and continue to cook the onion for about 10 minutes, stirring occasionally, until the liquid has evaporated and the onion is soft. Season to taste with salt and pepper.

Top the tarts with the greens and onion and serve warm.

leftover steak and fried egg tostadas with chipotle salsa

The main inspiration for making these tostadas should be the steak you have leftover from the night before. Of course, if you wanted to cook a steak just to make the tostadas, go right ahead.

SERVES 4

. . . .

2 tablespoons canola or safflower oil

4 corn tortillas

8 ounces cooked steak (such as rib-eye or New York strip steak), thinly sliced
Sea salt and freshly ground black pepper

1 tablespoon unsalted butter

1 tablespoon olive oil

4 large eggs
Chipotle Salsa (page 100)
Fresh cilantro leaves for garnish

1 avocado, pitted, peeled, and sliced

Try This!
If you don't have leftover steak, substitute other leftovers, like pork loin, pot roast, roasted chicken, or grilled shrimp or vegetables.

Heat the canola oil in a small skillet over medium-high heat. Place one tortilla in the oil and fry for about 30 seconds per side, until slightly crisp. Remove the tortilla to a paper towel to drain and repeat with the remaining tortillas. When all the tortillas are fried, pour out the oil.

Place the steak slices in the hot skillet for about 1 minute to warm them slightly.

Put the tortillas on a work surface or individual plates and lay the steak slices on them, dividing them evenly; season to taste with salt and pepper.

To fry the eggs, heat half of the butter with half of the olive oil in a large nonstick skillet over medium-high heat until hot. Crack 2 of the eggs into the skillet and fry the eggs for about 1 minute per side for over-easy, longer if you like your eggs more well done. Remove the eggs from the skillet and place 1 egg on top of each of 2 tostadas. Repeat, heating the remaining butter and oil and frying the remaining 2 eggs in the same way. Place them atop the remaining 2 tostadas.

Drizzle about 1 tablespoon of the Chipotle Salsa over each tostada, season with additional salt and pepper if desired, and scatter a few cilantro leaves and avocado slices over each. Serve warm, with extra salsa.

chilaquiles and andouille sausage scramble with salsa verde

This is the kind of egg dish that would satisfy even an eggs-for-dinner skeptic. Chilaquiles is a classic Mexican breakfast dish made of stale tortillas drenched in sauce (green sauce, red chile sauce, or mole), so the tortillas get a wonderful, slightly chewy texture. It's one of those dishes that every Mexican home cook makes a bit differently, improvising with what they have on hand.

SERVES 4 TO 6

- 4 corn tortillas, cut into 1-inch strips
- 1 tablespoon olive oil, plus more for brushing the tortillas
  Sea salt and freshly ground black pepper
- 2 andouille sausage links (about 8 ounces), thinly sliced into rounds

- 6 large eggs, lightly beaten
- 2 ounces Monterey Jack or pepper Jack cheese, shredded (about 1/2 cup)
  Salsa Verde (recipe follows)

Preheat the oven to 400°F.

Scatter the tortillas strips on a rimmed baking sheet and brush lightly with olive oil. Season to taste with salt and pepper and bake the tortilla strips for about 10 minutes, shaking the pan occasionally, until they're golden brown and crisp.

Heat the tablespoon of olive oil in a large nonstick skillet over medium-high heat. Add the sausage slices and cook and stir them for 4 to 5 minutes, until brown and cooked through. Pour the eggs into the skillet and cook, gently folding the eggs as they cook, until just done but still slightly wet looking. Season to taste with salt and pepper and turn off the heat. Add the cheese and tortilla strips to the skillet and fold them into the eggs until the cheese melts and the tortilla strips soften slightly. Drizzle the chilaquiles with 1/2 cup of the Salsa Verde and serve warm, with the remaining salsa on the side.

Quick Fix:

To skip the step of baking the tortillas, substitute 3 cups of tortilla chips for the tortillas in this recipe. You can also use your favorite bottled tomatillo or tomato salsa instead of making the Salsa Verde.

SALSA VERDE

Makes about 1¹/₂ cups

1 cup puréed canned tomatillos
   (with their juices)
¹/₂ cup fresh cilantro leaves
3 scallions, chopped (white and
   green parts)
2 garlic cloves, smashed
Juice of 1 lime
Sea salt and freshly ground
   black pepper

Combine the tomatillos and their
juices, cilantro, scallions, garlic, and
lime juice in a blender and purée
until smooth. Serve immediately, or
refrigerate in an airtight container
until ready to serve. Season with salt
and pepper.

smoked salmon toasts with poached eggs and dijon-dill sauce

Any breakfast that includes smoked salmon seems kind of elegant—and is guaranteed to be a hit at the Market.

SERVES 4

. . . .

DIJON-DILL SAUCE

- 1 tablespoon Dijon mustard
- 1 tablespoon mayonnaise
  Grated zest and juice of 1 lemon
- 2 tablespoons chopped fresh dill
- 4 tablespoons (½ stick) unsalted butter, melted and cooled slightly
  Sea salt and freshly ground black pepper

• • •

- 4 1-inch-thick slices crusty, rustic-style bread
  Olive oil for brushing the bread
- 1 teaspoon white vinegar
- 4 large eggs
- 4 ounces smoked salmon, thinly sliced (about 8 slices)
- 2 cups loosely packed watercress, tough stems removed

Preheat the broiler.

Stir the mustard, mayonnaise, lemon zest and juice, and dill together in a small bowl. Gradually whisk in the melted butter and season to taste with salt and pepper. Cover and keep warm.

Brush one side of the bread slices lightly with olive oil. Place oiled side up under the broiler for about 1 minute per side to toast lightly.

To poach the eggs, fill a deep skillet half-full with water. Add the vinegar, bring to a low boil over high heat, and reduce the heat so the water simmers. Break 1 egg into a small dish and carefully slide the egg into the simmering water. Repeat with the remaining eggs and poach them for about 2 minutes, spooning the poaching water over the tops of the eggs while they cook, until the egg whites are firm and the yolks are starting to set but are still soft in the center.

Remove the eggs with a slotted spoon, dab them on a paper towel to drain the excess water, and place one egg on each piece of toast. Lay the salmon slices over the eggs, dividing them evenly, and top each with ½ cup of watercress. Drizzle the sauce over and around the eggs and greens, season with additional salt and pepper if desired, and serve warm.

sara says_____
To eliminate the step of draining the eggs—and any risk of having the eggs fall apart—break each egg into a custard cup and place the cup into the pan of simmering water that comes just below the edge of the cup.

simple
suppers

THERE ARE TIMES when only a good old-fashioned-style entrée of meat, potatoes, and a vegetable will do. The recipes in this chapter, for lighter, fresher, and quicker ways of preparing familiar cuts of meat, are for those times. If you take advantage of quick-cooking cuts like beef fillet, sausage, chicken thighs, and lamb chops, all you need is a fast marinade and an easy-to-make, vibrantly flavored sauce or accompaniment to make them come alive and seem like a "finished" dish. Wherever possible, I give you "Quick Fix" options to save a step by buying a bottled sauce or other prepared food, but one place you don't want to take a shortcut is in the quality of the meats you use. Because these are such simple preparations, you want to start with high-quality, preferably organic ingredients like naturally raised, hormone-free beef, lamb, and pork, and free-range chicken. Trust me, you'll taste the difference.

curried chicken sauté

Boneless, skinless chicken breasts are what I cook most often, so I'm always experimenting with new ways to prepare them. This curry is one of the victories of that experimentation. The sauce is really rich so I recommend you serve it with something simple and clean tasting, like plain jasmine rice and steamed baby bok choy.

SERVES 4 TO 6

. . . .

4 boneless, skinless chicken breast halves, rinsed and patted dry
Sea salt and freshly ground black pepper
1 tablespoon unsalted butter
2 tablespoons olive oil
1 onion, diced
2 garlic cloves, minced
1 tablespoon curry powder
1 tablespoon grated peeled fresh ginger (from a 1-inch piece)

Grated zest and juice of 1 orange
1 cup unsweetened coconut milk
1 cup chicken broth
2 tablespoons mango chutney
1 tablespoon chopped fresh cilantro
1 tablespoon chopped fresh mint
¼ cup lightly toasted slivered almonds or unsalted cashews

sara says
When grating ginger, to prevent the ginger from getting stuck in the grater, wrap the grater with plastic wrap and grate on top of the plastic. The ginger comes right off.

Thinly slice the chicken breasts crosswise and season them all over with salt and pepper.

Heat the butter with the oil in a large skillet over medium-high heat until hot. Place the chicken strips in the skillet and sauté them for 3 to 4 minutes per side, until golden brown. Remove the chicken to a platter and cover loosely with foil to keep warm.

Reduce the heat to medium, add the onion, and sauté, stirring constantly, for 3 to 4 minutes, until tender and translucent. Add the garlic and sauté for about 1 minute, stirring constantly so it doesn't brown. Add the curry powder, ginger, orange zest and juice and stir, scraping the brown bits from the bottom of the skillet. Stir in the coconut milk and chicken broth and bring to a boil. Reduce the heat to low, return the chicken strips to the skillet, and simmer the chicken in the broth for 3 minutes to cook through. Stir in the chutney and cook the sauce for another minute to warm through. Sprinkle with the cilantro, mint, and almonds, and serve warm.

sautéed chicken and mushrooms with cheesy polenta and caramelized onion wedges

All you need to make this a meal is a green vegetable, like sautéed kale or spinach (see Garlic-Sautéed Spinach, page 202) or a crisp green salad.

SERVES 4

. . . .

1 red onion	4 boneless chicken breast halves
⅓ cup dry red wine	(skin on), rinsed and patted dry
2 tablespoons balsamic vinegar	Sea salt and freshly ground
2 tablespoons olive oil	black pepper
1 tablespoon chopped fresh	1 tablespoon unsalted butter
rosemary	8 ounces button or baby bella
1 tablespoon chopped fresh	mushrooms, wiped clean and
marjoram	stems trimmed
	Cheesy Polenta (see opposite)

Preheat the oven to 450°F.

Quarter the onion through the root end, leaving the root on to keep the quarters intact, and place them in an ovenproof skillet. Pour the wine and vinegar over the onion, drizzle with 1 tablespoon of the olive oil, and roast for about 30 minutes, until golden around the edges and tender, and the pan juices have thickened and caramelized.

Meanwhile, press the rosemary and marjoram into both sides of the chicken breasts and season them with salt and pepper. Heat the butter with the remaining tablespoon of olive oil in a large skillet over medium heat until hot. Place the chicken breasts skin side down in the skillet and cook for 5 to 6 minutes per side, until golden brown and cooked through. (If the chicken breasts are large and need more cooking time, place them in the oven to roast for about 5 minutes more.) Transfer the chicken breasts to a platter and cover them loosely with foil to keep warm.

Add the mushrooms to the skillet and sauté for 2 to 3 minutes, until golden brown. Remove the skillet from the heat and set aside.

To serve, divide the polenta evenly among four plates. Place one chicken breast atop each serving of polenta and drizzle it with the juices released on the platter they were resting on. Spoon the mushrooms and their liquid over the chicken; place one onion quarter, including some of the juices, on each plate.

sara says⎯⎯⎯⎯
I recommend cooking chicken with the skin on. The fat rendered from the skin adds essential flavor to the pan juices you'll cook the mushrooms in. Generally you won't find boneless, skin-on chicken sold at grocery stores, so either ask your butcher to cut the breasts off the bone or buy chicken breast halves and bone them yourself.

CHEESY POLENTA

2 cups chicken broth
2 cups whole milk
1 cup polenta
Sea salt
2 tablespoons unsalted butter
2 ounces Swiss cheese, shredded (about ½ cup)
⅔ cup freshly grated Parmesan cheese
Freshly ground black pepper

Combine the broth and milk in a large saucepan and bring to a boil over high heat. Reduce the heat to medium and add the polenta in a slow steady stream, whisking constantly until all the polenta is added and the mixture is smooth. Season to taste with salt, reduce the heat to low, and cook the polenta, stirring often, for 7 to 8 minutes, until it's thick and pulls away from the sides of the pan. Stir in the butter, Swiss cheese, and Parmesan cheese. Season to taste with pepper and additional salt if desired.

skewered thai chicken thighs with spicy peanut dipping sauce

The first time I tasted Thai food, I fell in love with satay—the skewered meat served with peanut sauce for dipping. I use chicken thighs for this version because their strong, gamy flavor stands up to the rich flavorful sauce. Note that you'll need eight long wooden or metal skewers to make this dish. To make it a complete meal, serve these skewers with a Classic Cucumber Salad (page 212) or Green Rice (page 220). *See photograph on page 144.*

SERVES 4 TO 6

- 8 boneless, skinless chicken thighs (about 1¾ pounds), rinsed and patted dry
- 2 tablespoons light soy sauce or tamari
- 2 tablespoons tamarind sauce or paste
- 1 tablespoon grated peeled fresh ginger (from a 1-inch piece)

- 2 garlic cloves, minced
- 2 scallions, minced (white and green parts)
- Sea salt and freshly ground black pepper
- Spicy Peanut Dipping Sauce (recipe follows)

sara says
If you're using wooden skewers, place them in a shallow baking dish, cover with water, and soak for 30 minutes.

Put the chicken thighs in a shallow glass bowl or large sealable plastic bag. Stir the soy sauce, tamarind sauce, ginger, garlic, and scallions together in a small bowl and pour over the chicken. Turn the chicken or shake the bag to coat the chicken with the marinade. Cover the bowl or close the bag and marinate the chicken for 30 minutes at room temperature or up to overnight in the refrigerator.

Prepare a hot fire in a charcoal or gas grill. (Or just before you're ready to cook the chicken, heat a grill pan or cast-iron skillet over medium-high heat until hot.)

Remove the chicken thighs from the marinade, season them with salt and pepper, and thread one thigh onto each skewer. Grill the chicken for 5 to 6 minutes per side, turning once and basting with the marinade while it cooks, until it's golden brown with dark grill marks. Move the chicken to the side of the grill, close the lid, and cook it for another 2 to 3 minutes, until cooked through. Remove the chicken to a platter and brush it lightly on all sides with the Spicy Peanut Dipping Sauce. Let the chicken rest, loosely covered with foil to keep warm, for about 5 minutes and serve with the remaining dipping sauce on the side.

SPICY PEANUT DIPPING SAUCE

¼ cup fresh cilantro (leaves and stems)
3 tablespoons smooth unsweetened peanut butter
2 tablespoons rice wine vinegar
2 tablespoons tamarind sauce or paste
2 tablespoons light soy sauce or tamari
1 tablespoon honey
1 tablespoon grated peeled fresh ginger (from a 1-inch piece)
2 garlic cloves, minced
Grated zest and juice of 1 orange
Grated zest and juice of 1 lemon
2 scallions, minced (white and green parts)
½ jalapeño pepper, cored, seeded, and minced
1 teaspoon crushed red pepper flakes

Combine the cilantro, peanut butter, vinegar, tamarind sauce, soy sauce, honey, ginger, garlic, orange zest and juice, lemon zest and juice, scallions, jalapeño pepper, and red pepper flakes in a blender or food processor and purée until smooth. Serve immediately, or refrigerate in an airtight container until ready to serve or for up to 1 week.

Quick Fix:
To save the step of making the dipping sauce, buy a good-quality bottled Thai peanut sauce or ask your local Thai restaurant to sell some.

Try This!
Use extra sauce to top grilled chicken breasts, dress a crisp green salad or cold noodles, or as a dipping sauce for a Crudité Platter (page 16).

poached chicken breasts with spring vegetables and horseradish

Both the chicken and the vegetables for this dish are cooked in broth, so it couldn't be healthier. I first made it one April to highlight the delicate flavors of the young spring vegetables I had found at the farmers' market.

SERVES 4

sara says

If you can't get baby vegetables, cut larger ones into 3-inch pieces.

Try This!

For a little extra kick, grate fresh horseradish over the top of the finished dish.

4 boneless, skinless chicken breast halves, rinsed and patted dry
Sea salt and freshly ground black pepper
4 cups chicken broth
6 black peppercorns
4 fresh thyme sprigs
2 bay leaves
1 lemon, halved
4 to 6 baby carrots, trimmed and scrubbed

4 to 6 small leeks, washed, drained, and cut into 3-inch pieces
4 to 6 baby radishes, trimmed and scrubbed
8 ounces pencil-thin asparagus, tough ends trimmed, cut into 3-inch pieces
6 ounces sugar snap peas or snow peas, stem ends and strings removed
¼ cup prepared horseradish for serving

Season both sides of the chicken breasts with salt and pepper.

Pour the chicken broth into a large pot and add the peppercorns, thyme, and bay leaves. Squeeze the juice from both halves of the lemon into the broth and drop the squeezed lemon halves into the broth. Bring the broth to a low boil over high heat. Add the chicken, carrots, leeks, and radishes; reduce the heat to low and simmer for 15 to 18 minutes. Add the asparagus and sugar snap peas, and cook for about 1 minute, until tender. Season to taste with salt and pepper.

To serve, place one chicken breast on each of four soup plates or bowls. Spoon the broth and vegetables over the chicken breasts and top each serving with a large dollop of horseradish.

pan-grilled beef fillet with marsala peppercorn sauce

Marsala is a fortified wine from Sicily similar to sherry or Madeira. It has a very distinctive flavor that makes for a wonderful, rich sauce with very little effort. I like this with a wedge of roasted squash.

SERVES 4

- 1 tablespoon plus 1 teaspoon olive oil
- 4 6-ounce beef fillets, about 1½ inches thick, at room temperature
  Sea salt
- 1 tablespoon black peppercorns
- 2 teaspoons green peppercorns
- 2 tablespoons fresh rosemary
- 2 shallots, thinly sliced
- ½ cup Marsala wine
- 1 tablespoon balsamic vinegar
- 2 tablespoons unsalted butter, cut into pieces

Rub 1 tablespoon of the olive oil into both sides of the steaks and season them with salt. Crush the black and green peppercorns with the flat side of a knife and press half of the peppercorns into both sides of the steaks, reserving the remaining peppercorns for the sauce. Sprinkle the rosemary on both sides of the steaks and press it into the meat.

Heat a large cast-iron skillet over medium heat until hot. Place the steaks in the skillet for 5 to 6 minutes per side, turning only once, for medium-rare, or until an instant-read thermometer registers 120°F. Remove the steaks to a platter, cover loosely with foil, and let them rest for about 5 minutes.

Heat the remaining teaspoon of olive oil over medium heat in the skillet you cooked the steaks in. Add the shallots and sauté for about 2 minutes just to soften them. Add the Marsala, vinegar, and the remaining black and green peppercorns, and simmer for about 2 minutes, until the liquid has reduced by half. Remove the skillet from the heat and whisk in the butter. Spoon the sauce over the steaks and serve warm.

backyard barbecued pork tenderloin

This pork tenderloin is a standard special at the Market. It's so tender that you can cut it without a knife, so it makes the perfect hot entrée to serve to guests who will be eating standing up. Our catering customers often request it sliced so they can serve it with dinner rolls or biscuits as an alternative to ham sandwiches. As a dinner entrée, I serve it with Cuban-inspired Spicy Black Beans (page 213).

SERVES 4 TO 6

. . . .

2 1-pound pork tenderloins

FOR THE MARINADE
1 cup spicy barbecue sauce
Grated zest and juice of
1 orange

2 tablespoons Worcestershire sauce
2 garlic cloves, minced
1 teaspoon crushed red pepper flakes

• • •

Whisk the barbecue sauce, orange zest and juice, Worcestershire sauce, garlic, and red pepper flakes together in a small bowl. Trim the fat and sinew from the tenderloins, rinse them, and pat dry. Place the tenderloins in a shallow glass bowl or in a large sealable bag. Pour the marinade over the tenderloins and turn the pork to coat the tenderloins. Cover the bowl and marinate the pork for 30 minutes at room temperature or up to overnight in the refrigerator.

Prepare a hot fire in a charcoal or gas grill.

Remove the tenderloins from the marinade and season on all sides with salt and pepper. Grill the tenderloins for about 15 minutes, basting with the marinade while cooking and turning them to cook all four sides. Move the tenderloins to the side of the grill, close the grill or cover the tenderloins with foil, and cook and baste for another 10 to 15 minutes, or until an instant-read thermometer inserted into the tenderloins reads 145°F for medium (longer, or until the thermometer reads 160°F, for medium-well pork). Let the tenderloins rest for about 5 minutes before slicing.

Thinly slice the tenderloin and divide the slices evenly among four plates.

BAKED SWEET POTATOES

4 medium sweet potatoes
Sea salt and freshly ground black
   pepper to taste
2 tablespoons olive oil
2 tablespoons chopped fresh cilantro
Juice of 1 lime

Preheat the oven to 400°F.

Scrub the sweet potatoes, wrap them individually in foil, and bake for about 40 minutes, until soft to the squeeze.

Stir the olive oil, cilantro, and lime juice together in a small bowl.

Cut a slit the length of the sweet potatoes, squeeze the potatoes to push the insides out a little, and put one sweet potato on each plate. Drizzle with the cilantro dressing, season to taste with salt and pepper, and serve.

grilled marinated lamb and pepper skewers

Lamb is ideal for last-minute meals. It has so much flavor that you really don't have to do much to it to make a great-tasting dinner. These skewers require little more than a quick marinade and a few minutes on the grill. Skewered meats, in my view, *must* be served on a bed of rice—in this case, either the Lemon-Coconut Basmati Rice Pilaf (page 221) or Green Rice (page 220). You'll need four long wooden or metal skewers to make these.

SERVES 4

FOR THE MARINADE

- 2 tablespoons olive oil
- 2 tablespoons chopped fresh oregano
- 1 tablespoon chopped fresh marjoram or flat-leaf parsley
- 2 garlic cloves, minced
  Juice of 1 lemon
- • • •

- 1 1½-pound trimmed boneless leg of lamb, at room temperature
  Sea salt and freshly ground black pepper
- 2 red bell peppers, cored, seeded, and cut into 2-inch chunks
- 1 lemon, quartered

To make the marinade, stir the olive oil, oregano, marjoram, garlic, and lemon juice together in a small bowl. Cut the lamb into 2-inch cubes and place in a shallow glass bowl or in a large sealable plastic bag. Pour the marinade over the lamb and turn the lamb or shake the bag to coat the meat with the marinade. Cover the bowl or close the bag and marinate the lamb for about 30 minutes at room temperature or up to overnight in the refrigerator.

Prepare a hot fire in a charcoal or gas grill.

Remove the lamb from the marinade and season it on all sides with salt and pepper. Thread the lamb and peppers onto four skewers, alternating between the two. Grill the skewers for 3 to 4 minutes on all four sides (for a total cooking time of 12 to 16 minutes for medium). Transfer the lamb skewers to a platter, cover them loosely with foil, and let rest for about 5 minutes before serving. Serve warm, with lemon wedges on the side.

Try This!
Serve the lamb skewers with toasted Syrian or pita bread and plain whole-milk yogurt for a casual lunch— or as a way to use leftovers.

sara says
When grilling meat, let it come to room temperature first for more even cooking.

maggie's curried lamb chops with curried mint yogurt sauce

Maggie is a friend who comes over occasionally to cook dinner for Peter and me. She tends to cook with ingredients that I don't normally use, like Indian spices, so her recipes stretch me out of my usual repertoire. In cold weather, I serve this with Cauliflower Purée (page 199), and on a hot day, with Cooley Tabbouleh (page 207).

SERVES 4 TO 6

sara says
Ask your butcher to French-trim the racks of lamb. French-trimming means cutting the meat and fat away from the bones, leaving about two inches of the bone clean and exposed.

¼ cup olive oil
1 tablespoon curry powder
1 tablespoon chopped fresh mint
1 tablespoon chopped fresh marjoram
  Grated zest of 1 orange
  Grated zest 1 lime

2 1½-pound racks of lamb (7 to 8 chops each), French trimmed, at room temperature
  Sea salt and freshly ground black pepper to taste
  Curried Mint Yogurt Sauce (recipe follows)

Preheat the oven to broil.

Stir the olive oil, curry powder, mint, marjoram, orange zest, and lime zest together in a small bowl to form a paste. Rub half of the paste into all sides of the lamb, pressing it into the fat to adhere.

Stand the lamb racks in a large roasting pan with the rib bones facing each other, propping each other up.

Place the lamb under the broiler for 3 to 4 minutes, until the outside is crisp; remove it from the oven and set aside for about 5 minutes. Cut the racks into individual chops, brush or rub the remaining paste into both sides of the chops, and season to taste with salt and pepper.

Heat a grill pan or cast-iron skillet over medium-high heat until hot. Put a few chops at a time in the pan to sear for about 1 minute per side for medium-rare (longer for the chops from the thick end of the rack). Remove the chops to a platter and set them aside to rest, loosely covered with foil, while you cook the remaining chops.

To serve, place three or four lamb chops on each plate. Spoon a dollop of the Curried Mint Yogurt Sauce over each serving.

Try This!
Serve with wedges of lemon and lime to squeeze over the lamb.

CURRIED MINT YOGURT SAUCE

1 cup plain whole-milk yogurt
1 tablespoon honey
2 tablespoons chopped fresh mint
2 teaspoons Dijon mustard
2 teaspoons curry powder
Juice of 1 lime
Sea salt and freshly ground
    black pepper

Stir the yogurt, honey, mint, mustard, curry powder, and lime juice together in a small bowl. Season to taste with salt and pepper and serve or cover and refrigerate until ready to serve.

rosemary-grilled boneless leg of lamb with tuscan white beans and roasted tomatoes

Ask your butcher for trimmed boneless leg of lamb, sometimes called leg loin. It may come in two or three pieces. This dish makes a fine, hearty supper as it is, but if it doesn't feel complete without a green vegetable, I would recommend something very simple, like Garlic-Sautéed Spinach (page 202).

SERVES 4

1 tablespoon olive oil

1 tablespoon chopped fresh rosemary

3 garlic cloves, smashed and chopped

1 1 ½-pound trimmed boneless leg of lamb, rinsed and patted dry

FOR THE BEANS

1 cup grape tomatoes or small cherry tomatoes

3 garlic cloves, smashed

1 tablespoon olive oil
Sea salt and freshly ground black pepper

1 15-ounce can cannellini beans or navy beans (about 2 cups), rinsed and drained

1 cup chicken broth

2 tablespoons chopped fresh rosemary

Quick Fix:
Use ½ cup of marinated sun-dried tomatoes in place of the roasted tomatoes. Adjust the amounts of garlic and olive oil accordingly.

Rub the olive oil, rosemary, and garlic over the leg of lamb, pressing the rosemary and garlic cloves into the meat. Set it aside to come to room temperature.

Preheat the oven to 350°F.

To make the beans, place the tomatoes and garlic on a rimmed baking sheet. Drizzle with the olive oil, season with salt and pepper, and toss to coat. Arrange the garlic so it's under the tomatoes to prevent it from burning. Roast for about 20 minutes, until the tomatoes are shriveled and burst in places.

Combine the beans, chicken broth, and rosemary in a small saucepan over medium-high heat and bring to a low boil. Reduce the heat, season to taste with salt and pepper, and simmer for about 5 minutes to bring out the flavor of the rosemary. Gently stir in the roasted tomatoes and garlic and simmer for about 5 minutes to meld the flavors. Remove the saucepan from the heat and keep warm.

Prepare a hot fire in a charcoal or gas grill.

Season the lamb with salt and pepper and grill 5 to 7 minutes per side, until an instant-read thermometer reads 125°F to 130°F for medium-rare. Remove the lamb to a cutting board, cover loosely with foil, and let it rest for about 5 minutes before slicing.

To serve, divide the beans and tomatoes evenly among four plates. Thinly slice the lamb, lay the slices on top of the beans, and pour the juices collected on the cutting board over the meat.

vegetarian eggplant rolls with savory tomato sauce and fresh ricotta cheese

I make these rolls often in the summer, when my garden is overloaded with eggplant.

SERVES 4

. . . .

- 2 tablespoons olive oil
- 2 tablespoons red wine vinegar
- 1 large eggplant, cut lengthwise into ¼-inch slices
  Sea salt and freshly ground black pepper
- 12 ounces fresh whole-milk ricotta cheese (about 1½ cups)
- ⅔ cup freshly grated Parmesan cheese, plus extra for sprinkling on the rolls
- 8 basil leaves, thinly sliced
  Savory Tomato Sauce (page 121)

Quick Fix:
To save the step of making the tomato sauce, use your favorite jarred tomato sauce instead.

Preheat the oven to 375°F.

Prepare a hot fire in a charcoal or gas grill. (Or just before you're ready to cook the eggplant, heat a grill pan or cast-iron skillet over medium-high heat until hot.)

Stir the olive oil and vinegar together in a small bowl and brush onto both sides of the eggplant slices; season both sides with salt and pepper. Grill the eggplant for 3 to 4 minutes per side, until tender and golden brown. Transfer the eggplant slices to a rimmed baking sheet with the short edges facing you.

Stir the ricotta cheese, Parmesan cheese, and half of the basil together in a medium bowl and season with salt and pepper. Spoon about 3 tablespoons of the cheese mixture onto each slice of eggplant about 1 inch from the bottom edge, leaving a ¼-inch border on each side. Roll each slice away from you and arrange the rolls seam side down on the baking sheet. Spoon the tomato sauce over the rolls and place them in the oven for about 15 minutes to warm through. Top with a sprinkling of Parmesan cheese and the remaining basil and serve warm.

my foolproof marinades

Even a short time in a marinade makes meat, chicken, or fish more moist, tender, and flavorful. It's best to have your seafood and meat at room temperature before cooking it, so if I'm marinating for a short enough time that whatever I'm marinating won't spoil, I marinate it at room temperature to accomplish two things at once. Suggested marinating times:

- VEGETABLES, TOFU, OR CHEESE: 20 to 30 minutes at room temperature.

- SEAFOOD: 5 to 10 minutes at room temperature or 1 hour in the refrigerator.

- POULTRY, PORK, LAMB, OR BEEF: 30 minutes to 1 hour at room temperature or overnight in the refrigerator.

Quick Fix:
To speed the marinating process, I often use a gadget called an instant marinator—a sealed plastic container with a pump to remove the air that gives the benefits of long marinating in as little as 15 minutes.

Balsamic Red Wine Marinade

Stir together ¼ cup red wine, 2 tablespoons balsamic vinegar, 1 tablespoon olive oil, 1 tablespoon Worcestershire sauce, 2 tablespoons chopped fresh rosemary, 2 minced garlic cloves, and a few turns of freshly ground black pepper.

GOOD WITH: steak, pork, or lamb chops.

Herb Marinade

Stir together ¼ cup white wine, 2 tablespoons olive oil, the zest and juice of 1 lemon, ¼ cup chopped fresh herbs (rosemary, thyme, oregano, sage, or a combination), and 3 minced garlic cloves.

GOOD WITH: fish, shrimp, scallops, chicken, vegetables, or cheese.

Sweet and Spicy Marinade

Stir together 2 tablespoons soy sauce, 1 tablespoon apple cider vinegar, the zest and juice of 1 orange, 2 tablespoons chopped fresh cilantro, 1 tablespoon grated peeled fresh ginger, 1 tablespoon honey, 1 minced scallion (white and green parts), 2 minced garlic cloves, and 1 teaspoon crushed red pepper flakes.

GOOD WITH: salmon, shrimp, chicken, turkey, or pork.

Hoisin Marinade

Stir together ¼ cup hoisin sauce, 2 tablespoons soy sauce, the zest and juice of 1 orange, 1 tablespoon light brown sugar, 2 minced garlic cloves, 2 minced scallions (white and green parts), and $\frac{1}{2}$ teaspoon crushed red pepper flakes.

GOOD WITH: pork, chicken, duck, or lamb.

Curry Marinade

Stir together 2 tablespoons rice wine vinegar, 2 tablespoons curry powder, the zest and juice of 1 orange, the zest and juice of 1 lime, 1 tablespoon grated peeled fresh ginger, 2 minced garlic cloves, 1 tablespoon honey, and freshly ground black pepper.

GOOD WITH: fish, shrimp, tofu, grilled vegetables, chicken, pork, or duck.

Mixed Herb Mustard Marinade

Stir together $\frac{1}{4}$ cup red wine, 2 tablespoons Dijon mustard, 2 tablespoons olive oil, 2 tablespoons chopped fresh rosemary, 1 tablespoon chopped fresh marjoram or flat-leaf parsley, and freshly ground black pepper.

GOOD WITH: steak, pork tenderloin, lamb, or grilled potatoes.

Tandoori Marinade

Stir together 1 cup plain yogurt, 1 diced red onion, 1 teaspoon ground cumin, 1 teaspoon turmeric, 1 tablespoon honey, 2 tablespoons chopped fresh cilantro, and the zest and juice of 1 lemon.

GOOD WITH: lamb, chicken, or eggplant (to cook on the grill).

Fruit and Herb Marinade

Stir together 1 cup unfiltered apple juice, 2 tablespoons olive oil, 2 minced shallots, 2 minced garlic cloves, 1 tablespoon fresh thyme, sage, and/or rosemary, and $\frac{1}{4}$ cup dried cherries or cranberries.

GOOD WITH: pork, duck, turkey, or chicken.

Sesame Peanut Marinade

Combine the zest and juice of 1 orange, 2 tablespoons rice wine vinegar, 2 minced scallions, 2 minced garlic gloves, 1 tablespoon grated peeled fresh ginger, 1 tablespoon peanut butter, and 1 tablespoon sesame oil in a blender and purée until smooth.

GOOD WITH: chicken, pork, or beef; or tofu or eggplant (to be grilled).

three easy ways to turn sausage into dinner

There are many wonderful varieties of sausage to choose from, including some that are nitrate-free and made from premium-quality pork, beef, and lamb, and lower-fat sausages made with turkey, chicken, or seafood. I like to keep a few varieties in the freezer for quick dinners, like these:

Italian Sausage Soup

A big bowl of this hearty soup hits the spot on a cold winter night. All you need to make it a meal is warm crusty bread or Toasted Garlic Bread (page 36).

SERVES 4

1 pound Italian pork sausage (spicy or sweet)

1 onion, chopped

3 cups chicken broth

1 14.5-ounce can chopped tomatoes (with their juices)

1 cup orecchiette (ear-shaped pasta)

Sea salt and freshly ground black pepper

4 cups loosely packed spinach, washed, drained, and trimmed of tough stems

4 basil leaves, thinly sliced

Quick Fix:
To save the step of cooking the pasta (or if you prefer beans to pasta), substitute a 15-ounce can of cannellini beans or navy beans for the orecchiette in this recipe.

Cut open the sausage casings and squeeze the meat into a large skillet over medium-high heat, discarding the casings. Add the onion and sauté the sausage and onion for about 5 minutes, stirring occasionally, until the sausage is light brown all over and the onion tender and translucent. Drain the fat from the skillet, and add the chicken broth, tomatoes (with their juices), and pasta; season to taste with salt and pepper, and bring to a boil. Reduce the heat and simmer the soup for 8 to 10 minutes, until the pasta is al dente. Turn off the heat and stir in the spinach and basil. Season with additional salt and pepper if desired and serve warm.

Open-Faced Chicken Sausage Sandwiches

This is my idea of a perfect one-dish dinner: savory sausage, crusty bread, and a pile of greens—a bit of each in every bite.

SERVES 4

2 tablespoons olive oil

2 tablespoons balsamic vinegar

2 tablespoons chopped fresh oregano, marjoram, or flat-leaf parsley

2 red bell peppers, cored, seeded, and cut into 1-inch pieces

1 onion, cut into 1-inch chunks
Sea salt and freshly ground black pepper

1 pound chicken sausage or Italian pork sausage (spicy or sweet), cut into 1-inch chunks

4 1-inch thick slices crusty, rustic-style bread

2 tablespoons whole-grain mustard

4 cups loosely packed mixed baby greens, washed and drained

Prepare a hot fire in a charcoal or gas grill. If you're using wooden skewers, place them in a shallow baking dish, cover with water, and soak for 30 minutes.

Whisk the olive oil, vinegar, and oregano together in a small bowl. Put the peppers and onion in a medium bowl and drizzle half the vinaigrette over the vegetables, reserving the remaining vinaigrette to dress the sandwich. Season with salt and pepper and toss to coat.

Thread the peppers, onion, and sausage onto skewers, alternating ingredients. Grill the skewers for about 8 minutes, turning them every 2 minutes for even browning, until the sausage is cooked through and the peppers and onion are slightly soft.

Place the bread slices on the grill for about 1 minute per side, until lightly toasted. Spread one side of each slice lightly with mustard. Drizzle the greens with the remaining vinaigrette, season to taste with salt and pepper, and toss to coat.

Remove the vegetables and sausage from the skewers, and arrange on the toasts. Top each with a mound of greens.

Spaghetti with Quick Bolognese

Bolognese is traditionally made with ground beef, pork, veal, or a combination, cooked long and slow. Here is my quick version, using sausage in place of the ground meats. Serve it with a crisp green salad.

SERVES 4 TO 6

1 tablespoon olive oil

1 onion, diced

1 carrot, diced

1 pound Italian pork sausage (spicy or sweet)

4 garlic cloves, minced

½ teaspoon crushed red pepper flakes

Sea salt and freshly ground black pepper

2 tablespoons tomato paste

½ cup dry red wine

1 28-ounce can chopped tomatoes (with their juices)

¼ cup heavy cream or milk

2 tablespoons chopped fresh oregano, marjoram, or flat-leaf parsley

Kosher salt

8 ounces spaghetti

⅓ cup freshly grated Parmesan cheese, plus more for passing

Heat the olive oil in a large skillet over medium heat. Add the onion and sauté for 3 to 4 minutes, until tender and translucent. Add the carrot and cook for about 2 minutes, until it softens slightly. Cut the sausage casings and squeeze the meat into the skillet, discarding the casings. Add the garlic and red pepper flakes, season with salt and pepper, and cook and stir for another 3 to 4 minutes, breaking up the sausage with a spoon as it cooks, until light brown but not cooked through. Add the tomato paste and stir to combine thoroughly. Add the wine and simmer for about 2 minutes to reduce it slightly. Add the tomatoes (and their juices), reduce the heat to low, and simmer the sauce, partially covered, for about 30 minutes to thicken. Turn off the heat and stir in the heavy cream and oregano.

Meanwhile, bring a large pot of water to a boil and add salt. Stir in the spaghetti and cook until al dente, 8 to 9 minutes, or according to the package directions. Reserve a cupful of the pasta cooking water, drain the spaghetti, and add it to the pan with the sauce. Toss to coat and add enough of the reserved water to make the sauce slippery. Sprinkle the pasta with Parmesan and pass more at the table.

fish in a flash

Sweet-'n'-Sour Shrimp

Chipotle Shrimp Scampi

Shrimp Chilaquiles with Salsa Verde

Steamed Clams with White Wine and
Fresh Herbs

Pan-Seared Sea Scallops with
Corn Coulis

Pan-Seared Salmon with Sweet and
Spicy Asian Glaze

Pan-Seared Halibut with Sautéed
Sweet Peppers and Olive-Caper Relish

Pan-Roasted Cod with Sautéed
Chanterelle Mushrooms

Seared Tuna Tartare with Jalapeño
Peppers, Cilantro, and Avocado

FISH COOKS QUICKLY so it's the ideal choice when you want to get dinner on the table and *fast*. A lot of people are intimidated by the idea of cooking fish because they don't know how to dress it, but in fact, most fish are so delicate in flavor that a lot of seasoning is overkill. In these recipes, you'll see how just a simple touch—smoky chipotle peppers added to shrimp scampi, a sweet pepper, caper, and olive relish to top halibut fillets, or a sweet and spicy marinade cooked down until it forms a glaze for pan-seared salmon—is all you need to transform fish into a special dish. Because it's an absolute must to use fresh fish, these recipes do require a trip to the market, but that trip to the market won't seem like a big deal when you realize it's the hardest part of making dinner. Although I call for specific types of fish in these recipes, use whatever varieties you have access to that are fresh (never frozen) and preferably caught locally. Otherwise, forget it, and grill a steak instead.

sweet-'n'-sour shrimp

This sweet-'n'-sour shrimp is a lot less sweet and not nearly as fluorescent as what you get in most Chinese restaurants. Serve it over a bed of steamed jasmine rice or rice noodles to catch all the delicious sauce.

SERVES 4

. . . .

FOR THE MARINADE

½ cup sake or sweet white wine

2 tablespoons spicy pepper jelly

2 tablespoons rice wine vinegar

1 tablespoon Thai chili paste

1 tablespoon light soy sauce

Juice of 1 lime

. . .

2 pounds large shrimp, peeled and deveined

1 tablespoon unsalted butter

1 tablespoon olive oil

2 shallots, minced

Sea salt and freshly ground black pepper

2 roasted red bell peppers (see "Roasting Peppers," page 79; or from a jar or deli case)

2 garlic cloves, minced

¼ cup fresh cilantro leaves

To make the marinade, whisk the sake, pepper jelly, vinegar, chili paste, soy sauce, and lime juice together in a medium bowl. Add the shrimp and turn to coat. Cover the bowl and marinate the shrimp for 15 minutes.

Melt half of the butter with the half of the olive oil in a large skillet over medium-high heat. Add half of the shallots and sauté for about 2 minutes, stirring often, to soften them. Add half of the shrimp to the skillet, and season them with salt and pepper. Sauté the shrimp for about 30 seconds per side, until they just begin to turn pink. Transfer the shrimp to a platter, cover loosely with foil to keep warm, and repeat the process, reserving the marinade.

Add the roasted peppers and the garlic to the skillet you cooked the shrimp in and sauté for about 1 minute, stirring constantly to prevent the garlic from browning. Add the marinade and simmer it for about 2 minutes to reduce and thicken it slightly. Return the shrimp and the juices that have collected on the plate to the skillet and cook and stir for about 1 minute, until the shrimp are warmed through and coated with the sauce. Sprinkle with the cilantro, and serve warm.

chipotle shrimp scampi

My friends Harry and Diane serve a version of this at their Mexican restaurant in Saranac Lake, near Lake Placid. In keeping with the south-of-the-border theme, I serve it with warm tortillas. Cool down the heat of the chipotle peppers by passing a plate of avocado slices drizzled with lime juice and sprinkled with sea salt.

SERVES 4 TO 6

- 2 tablespoons olive oil
- 2 pounds large shrimp, peeled and deveined
  Sea salt and freshly ground black pepper
- 2 garlic cloves, minced
- 1 chipotle chile in adobo, minced
- ½ cup dry white wine
  Grated zest and juice of 1 lemon
- 2 tablespoons chopped fresh cilantro
- 4 to 8 flour or corn tortillas, warmed (see "Warming Tortillas," page 97)

Heat 1 tablespoon of the olive oil in a large skillet over medium-high heat until it's hot. Add half of the shrimp, season with salt and pepper, and sauté for about 30 seconds per side, until they just begin to turn pink. Add half of the garlic and half of the chipotle and cook and stir about 1 minute more, until the shrimp are completely pink and cooked through. Remove the shrimp to a plate and cover loosely to keep warm. Repeat, heating the remaining oil and cooking the remaining shrimp, garlic, and chipotle in the same way. Remove the second batch of shrimp to the plate.

Add the wine to the skillet you cooked the shrimp in and simmer over medium heat for about 1 minute to reduce slightly. Return the shrimp and the juices collected on the plate they were resting on to the skillet. Add the lemon zest and juice and cook and stir for about 1 minute to combine the ingredients and coat the shrimp with the sauce. Remove from the heat, stir in the cilantro, and season with additional salt and pepper, if desired.

To serve, divide the shrimp evenly among four plates, spoon the sauce over them, and serve the warm tortillas on the side.

shrimp chilaquiles with salsa verde

These chilaquiles are topped with queso fresco, a soft fresh Mexican cow's milk cheese that gives them a distinctive Mexican flavor.

SERVES 4

. . . .

- 4 corn tortillas, cut into 1-inch strips
- 1 tablespoon olive oil, plus extra for brushing the tortillas
  Sea salt and freshly ground black pepper
- 1 pound large shrimp, peeled and deveined
- 2 garlic cloves, minced
- 1 jalapeño pepper, cored, seeded, and minced

- ½ cup dry white wine
- ½ cup heavy cream
- 1 cup Salsa Verde (page 141; or from a jar or canned puréed tomatillos)
- 4 ounces queso fresco, crumbled (fresh Mexican cheese or goat cheese; about 1 cup)
- ¼ cup chopped fresh cilantro
- 2 tablespoons finely chopped onion

Preheat the oven to 400°F.

Scatter the tortilla strips on a rimmed baking sheet and brush them lightly with olive oil. Season with salt and pepper and bake for about 10 minutes, shaking the pan occasionally, until they're golden brown and crisp.

Heat the olive oil in a large skillet over medium-high heat until hot. Add the shrimp, season with salt and pepper, and sauté for about 30 seconds per side, until they just begin to turn pink. Add the garlic and jalapeño pepper and sauté for 1 minute, stirring constantly so the garlic doesn't brown. Transfer the shrimp and vegetables to a plate.

Add the wine to the skillet and simmer over medium-high heat to reduce slightly. Add the cream and simmer the sauce for about 2 minutes to thicken. Return the shrimp and their juices to the skillet. Pour the salsa over the shrimp and sprinkle with the queso fresco. Cover the pan, remove from the heat, and let sit for about 1 minute, until the cheese melts.

To serve, pile the tortilla strips on four plates. Pour the sauce and shrimp over them, and sprinkle with the cilantro and chopped onion.

steamed clams with white wine and fresh herbs

If you make this in a cast-iron skillet, bring the rustic skillet right to the table for people to dig in, family style; it looks beautiful. You can make this recipe with mussels in place of the clams. A lightly dressed green salad completes the meal.

SERVES 4

· ·

- 1 cup dry white wine or rosé wine
- 2 tablespoons olive oil
- 2 tablespoons unsalted butter
- 2 garlic cloves, smashed
- 6 black peppercorns
  Sea salt and freshly ground black pepper
- 1 pound small clams (such as littleneck or Maine clams), rinsed and scrubbed

- 6 fresh oregano sprigs
- 6 fresh parsley sprigs
- 1 small fresh red or green chile, thinly sliced
- 1 lemon, halved
  Crusty, rustic-style sourdough bread or baguette, warmed

Combine the wine, olive oil, butter, garlic, peppercorns, and salt and pepper in a large skillet with a tight-fitting lid over high heat and bring to a boil, uncovered. Add the clams, oregano, parsley, chile, and lemon. Cover, and cook for 2 minutes. Uncover the skillet, remove any opened clams to a bowl, cover again, and cook the remaining clams for another minute, opening the pot periodically to remove any opened clams. After the clams have cooked for about 4 minutes, discard any clams that remain unopened.

Return the opened clams to the skillet, cover, and cook just until they're warmed through. Serve the clams with bowls for discarding the shells and the warm bread on the side for dipping into the broth.

pan-seared sea scallops with corn coulis

Although scallops are available year-round, they're actually a
summertime delicacy and especially sweet at that time.

SERVES 4 TO 6

. . . .

2 pounds sea scallops, rinsed and
  patted dry
  Sea salt and freshly ground
  black pepper
2 tablespoons unsalted butter
2 tablespoons olive oil
1 shallot, minced
1 garlic clove, minced

¼ cup dry white wine
  Kernels cut from 3 ears of corn
  (about 1½ cups)
¼ cup heavy cream
4 fresh basil leaves, thinly sliced
2 tablespoons chopped
  fresh chives

❧
Quick Fix:
To save the time it
takes to cut the
corn from the cob,
or to make this
when fresh corn
isn't in season, use
1½ cups of frozen
corn in place of
fresh corn kernels.
Look for organic
corn, which tends to
be sweeter than
conventional brands.

Remove the muscle from each scallop and season both sides with salt
and pepper.

Heat 1 tablespoon of the butter with 1 tablespoon of the olive oil in a
large nonstick skillet over medium-high heat until hot. Place half of the
scallops in the pan and sear for 1 to 1½ minutes per side, until golden
brown. Remove the scallops to a plate and cover them loosely with
foil to keep warm. Repeat the process, heating the remaining butter and
oil and cooking the remaining scallops in the same way.

Reduce the heat to medium, add the shallot and garlic to the skillet you
cooked the scallops in, and cook and stir about 1 minute to soften.
Add the wine and scrape the brown bits from the bottom of the skillet.
Add the corn, cream, basil, and chives and cook, stirring often, for
about 3 minutes, to reduce and thicken the cream slightly; season to
taste with salt and pepper. Transfer half of the sauce to a blender and
purée until smooth. Return the puréed sauce to the skillet, add the
scallops and the liquid collected on the plate they were resting on, and
cook just to warm the scallops—no more than a minute.

To serve, divide the scallops evenly among four plates and spoon the
sauce over and around them. Serve warm.

pan-seared salmon with sweet and spicy asian glaze

Salmon is one of those foods, like a boneless and skinless chicken breast, that everyone seems to like. This Asian-inspired marinade gives the tried-and-true fish new life.

SERVES 4

sara says_____
Look for wild salmon. Not only does it taste a lot better than conventional salmon, it's better for you and better for the oceans.

FOR THE MARINADE

2 tablespoons light soy sauce

2 tablespoons olive oil
  Juice of 1 orange

3 tablespoons rice wine vinegar

1 small fresh red or green chile, thinly sliced

1 tablespoon grated peeled fresh ginger (from a 1-inch piece)

• • •

4 6-ounce salmon fillets, about 1½ inches thick (skin on)
  Sea salt and freshly ground black pepper

2 tablespoons olive oil

2 tablespoons fresh cilantro leaves

To make the marinade, stir the soy sauce, olive oil, orange juice, vinegar, chile, and ginger together in a small bowl. Place the salmon fillets in a shallow glass dish, pour the marinade over the fillets, and turn them to coat the fillets. Cover and marinate for at least 30 minutes.

Remove the salmon from the marinade, reserving the marinade, and season both sides with salt and pepper. Heat the olive oil in a large nonstick skillet over medium-high heat until hot. Place the salmon fillets skin side down in the skillet to cook for 3 to 4 minutes per side, until golden brown and cooked through. Remove the salmon to a platter and cover loosely with foil to keep warm.

Pour the reserved marinade into the skillet and simmer for 2 to 3 minutes, until thick and syrupy. Drizzle the salmon fillets with the glaze, sprinkle them with the cilantro leaves, and serve.

pan-seared halibut with sautéed sweet peppers and olive-caper relish

This is the kind of fish dish I imagine I'd be served in a seaside village in Sicily. The salty, slightly bitter relish provides the perfect contrast to the sweet peppers.

SERVES 4

- 2 tablespoons olive oil
- 2 red or yellow bell peppers, cored, seeded, and julienned
- 1 red onion, thinly sliced
- 6 fresh basil leaves, thinly sliced
- 4 6-ounce halibut or grouper fillets, about 1½ inches thick
  Sea salt and freshly ground black pepper

FOR THE RELISH
- 6 large green Spanish olives, pitted
- 2 tablespoons capers, drained
- 2 garlic cloves
  Juice of 1 lemon
- 1 tablespoon olive oil
  Sea salt and freshly ground black pepper

Heat 1 tablespoon of the olive oil in a large nonstick skillet over medium-high heat until hot. Add the peppers and onion and sauté until the vegetables are slightly softened, about 2 minutes. Stir in half the basil, transfer the mixture to a bowl, and cover loosely with foil to keep warm.

Rub the halibut fillets on both sides with the remaining tablespoon of olive oil and remaining basil and season both sides with salt and pepper. Place the fillets skin side down in the skillet you cooked the peppers and onion in and cook over medium-high heat for 3 to 4 minutes per side, until golden brown and cooked through.

To make the relish, combine the olives, capers, garlic, lemon juice, and olive oil in a mortar and pestle and smash lightly to form a chunky paste. Season to taste with salt and pepper.

To serve, spread the peppers and onion on a serving platter or four dinner plates, dividing them evenly. Place the fish on top of the vegetables and spoon the olive-caper relish over the fish.

pan-roasted cod with sautéed chanterelle mushrooms

Cod is an underappreciated fish. It has a wonderful silky texture and mild, almost buttery flavor that is just delicious. The mushrooms are rich and flavorful, so serve the fish on a bed of wilted spinach to keep it light.

SERVES 4

- 3 tablespoons olive oil
- 4 6-ounce cod fillets, about 1½ inches thick (skin on, scales off), rinsed and patted dry
  Sea salt and freshly ground black pepper
- 4 tablespoons (½ stick) unsalted butter
- 4 ounces chanterelle mushrooms, wiped clean and sliced
- 1 shallot, minced
- ¼ cup dry white wine
  Juice of 1 lemon
- 2 tablespoons chopped fresh chives

Heat 1 tablespoon of the olive oil in a large nonstick skillet over medium-high heat. Season the cod fillets with salt and pepper on both sides and place skin side down in the skillet to cook for 3 to 4 minutes, until golden brown and crisp. Flip the fillets and cook for another 3 to 4 minutes, until golden brown and cooked through. Remove the fillets to a platter and cover them loosely with foil to keep warm.

Meanwhile, heat 2 tablespoons of the butter with the remaining 2 tablespoons of olive oil in the skillet you cooked the fish in over medium-high heat. Add the mushrooms and shallot, and cook and stir until the mushrooms are golden, about 2 minutes. Add the wine and lemon juice, bring to a boil, and boil for about 1 minute to reduce it slightly. Remove the skillet from the heat. Cut the remaining 2 tablespoons of butter into small pieces, drop them into the pan, and swirl the pan until the sauce is creamy. Serve the fish fillets with the mushrooms spooned over and around them and chives sprinkled on top.

sara says———
Wipe the mushrooms clean rather than rinsing them under water, which will make them soggy.

seared tuna tartare with jalapeño peppers, cilantro, and avocado

I make this tartare for guests because it seems fancy—only I know how easy it is to make. Searing the tuna gives it a charred, smoky flavor. Serve it on crostini (see Herbed Crostini, page 37) or endive leaves as an hors d'oeuvre, or with a crisp green salad as a light, healthy meal. Tartare is all about freshness, so when corn isn't in season, I leave the corn out rather than substitute frozen. You can cook the tuna on an outdoor grill instead of a grill pan; if you do, grill the corn rather than boiling it.

SERVES 4 TO 6

- 1 ear of corn, silks and husk removed
- 12 ounces ahi tuna steak, about 1 inch thick, rinsed and patted dry
- 2 tablespoons extra-virgin olive oil
  Sea salt and freshly ground black pepper
- ¼ cup chopped fresh cilantro
- 4 fresh basil leaves, thinly sliced

- 2 scallions, minced (white and green parts)
- 1 jalapeño pepper, cored, seeded, and minced
- 2 teaspoons hot sauce, such as Texas Pete or Tabasco
  Grated zest and juice of 1 lime
- 1 avocado, halved, pitted, peeled, and cut into small dice

Cook the corn in a pot of boiling water for 2 to 3 minutes, until the kernels are tender. Drain, let the corn cool to room temperature, and then cut the kernels off the cob.

Brush the tuna with 1 tablespoon of the olive oil and season both sides with salt and pepper. Heat a cast-iron skillet or grill pan over medium-high heat until hot. Place the tuna in the skillet to sear for 1 minute per side. Transfer the tuna to a cutting board to cool to room temperature.

Finely chop the tuna and transfer it to a medium bowl. Drizzle with the remaining tablespoon of olive oil. Add the corn kernels, cilantro, basil, scallions, jalapeño pepper, hot sauce, and lime zest and juice; season the tartare with salt and pepper to taste and toss to combine. Just before serving, add the avocado and toss again gently.

FISH IN A FLASH

fast and easy
side dishes

OFTEN TIMES WHEN YOU'RE preparing a meal, it's the side dishes that take all the time. Well, not these. I have a thing for sides, so much so that I sometimes let the sides determine what I make for dinner. (I love to make a dinner out of nothing but sides—doesn't everybody?) For the most part, the dishes in this chapter are classics with a twist. Baked potatoes are made from small Yukon Gold potatoes and a touch of basil livens up the flavor of my sister Judy's tried-and-true creamed corn. The selection of recipes here is a mix of year-round favorites, like Broccoli Rabe with White Beans or any of the rice or legume dishes, and seasonal favorites, like the Mixed Bean and Sweet Pepper Salad, so you'll have plenty to choose from any time of the year.

judy's creamed corn

I learned to make this from my nephew, Patrick, who works with me at the Market. It's a recipe from his mom, my sister Judy, and it's his all-time favorite vegetable dish. Judy wouldn't think of making it with anything but sweet summer corn.

SERVES 4 TO 6

- 6 ears of corn, husks and silks removed
- 3 tablespoons unsalted butter
  Sea salt and freshly ground black pepper
- 2 tablespoons cornstarch
- 2 tablespoons sugar
- 3 fresh basil leaves, thinly sliced

Cut the kernels off the cobs into a large bowl and scrape the cobs with the back of the knife to release the juice and pulp into the bowl.

Heat the butter in a large skillet over medium heat. Add the corn, season it with salt and pepper, and cook for about 2 minutes, stirring often, until it softens slightly.

Stir the cornstarch into $\frac{1}{2}$ cup of water and add it to the skillet with the corn. Add another $1\frac{1}{2}$ cups of water and bring to a boil over high heat. Reduce the heat and simmer the corn for about 3 minutes, until the sauce thickens. Stir in the sugar and season with additional salt and pepper to taste. Stir in the fresh basil and serve.

broccoli rabe with white beans

Escarole and beans is a classic Italian combination. I use broccoli rabe in place of the escarole. Depending on what you're serving this with, you may want to finish it with finely chopped onion or serve it with lemon wedges in place of the Parmesan cheese. Because beans are so hearty, I could make a dinner of this with Toasted Garlic Bread (page 36).

SERVES 4 TO 6

Kosher salt
1 bunch broccoli rabe, trimmed of tough ends (about 1½ pounds)
1 tablespoon unsalted butter
2 tablespoons olive oil
4 garlic cloves, minced

1 15-ounce can cannellini beans or navy beans, rinsed and drained (about 2 cups)
1 cup chicken or vegetable broth
Sea salt and freshly ground black pepper
⅓ cup freshly grated Parmesan cheese

Good with:
Grilled Marinated Lamb and Pepper Skewers (page 159), Pan-Seared Halibut with Sautéed Sweet Peppers and Olive-Caper Relish (page 187), or Arugula and Spinach Salad with Prosciutto, Pears, and Pecorino Cheese (page 51).

Bring a medium pot of water to a boil and add salt. Add the broccoli rabe and blanch for 10 to 15 seconds, until it turns bright green. Drain the broccoli, rinse it under cold water until completely cooled, and drain again.

Heat the butter with the olive oil in a large skillet over medium heat until hot. Add the garlic and sauté for about 1 minute, stirring constantly so it doesn't brown. Add the beans and broth, season to taste with salt and pepper, and cook, stirring occasionally, for about 5 minutes. Add the broccoli rabe, stir to combine, and cook until all the ingredients are warmed through, about 2 minutes. Serve warm, sprinkled with the Parmesan cheese.

vegetable purées

Puréed vegetables are so warm and comforting; they're like grown-up baby food. You can make vegetable purées from just about any vegetable: winter squash, turnips, rutabagas, parsnips, beets, sweet potatoes, green peas, edamame, or lima beans. These are some I make a lot. *See photograph on page 193.*

EACH SERVES 4 TO 6

Carrot Purée

1 pound carrots, chopped	Juice of 1 orange
3 tablespoons unsalted butter	1 tablespoon fresh thyme
1 tablespoon olive oil	Sea salt and freshly ground
1 cup chicken or vegetable broth	black pepper

Place the carrots, 1 tablespoon of the butter, the olive oil, chicken broth, and orange juice in a saucepan and bring to a boil over high heat. Reduce the heat to medium, cover, and cook the carrots for about 20 minutes, until tender. Purée the carrots in a food processor with the remaining 2 tablespoons butter, thyme, and 2 to 3 tablespoons of the liquid the carrots were cooked in (or more if necessary to make a smooth purée), until smooth. Season the purée to taste with salt and pepper and serve warm.

GOOD WITH: Pan-Roasted Cod with Sautéed Chanterelle Mushrooms (page 189) or Sweet-'n'-Sour Shrimp (page 175).

Broccoli Purée

1 head broccoli, trimmed and cut or broken into bite-size florets	2 tablespoons heavy cream
3 tablespoons unsalted butter	2 scallions, chopped (white and green parts)
1 tablespoon olive oil	Sea salt and freshly ground
½ cup chicken or vegetable broth	black pepper
½ cup freshly grated Parmesan cheese	

Place the broccoli, 1 tablespoon of the butter, the olive oil, and broth in a saucepan and bring to a boil over high heat. Reduce the heat to medium, cover, and cook the broccoli for about 7 minutes, until bright green and just tender. Purée the broccoli in a food processor with the remaining 2 tablespoons butter, the Parmesan cheese, cream, and scallions until smooth. Season the purée to taste with salt and pepper and serve warm.

GOOD WITH: Rosemary-Grilled Boneless Leg of Lamb with Tuscan White Beans and Roasted Tomatoes (page 162) or Curried Chicken Sauté (page 147).

Cauliflower Purée

- 1 head of cauliflower (about 1½ pounds), cut or broken into bite-size florets
- 1 cup chicken or vegetable broth
  Sea salt and freshly ground black pepper
- 3 tablespoons unsalted butter, cut into small pieces

- 1 tablespoon heavy cream
- 1 tablespoon chopped fresh flat-leaf parsley, plus extra for garnish
- 1 tablespoon chopped fresh chives, plus extra for garnish

Place the cauliflower florets in a large saucepan. Add the broth, season with salt and pepper, and bring the broth to a boil over high heat. Reduce the heat to low, cover, and simmer the cauliflower for 8 to 10 minutes, until tender. Remove the cauliflower with a slotted spoon. Purée in a food processor with the butter, cream, and 2 to 3 tablespoons of the broth you cooked the cauliflower in (or enough to make a smooth purée) until smooth. Add the parsley and chives, season to taste with additional salt and pepper, and pulse just to combine the ingredients. Serve warm, topped with a sprinkling of parsley and chives.

GOOD WITH: Pan-Grilled Beef Fillet with Marsala Peppercorn Sauce (page 155) or Maggie's Curried Lamb Chops with Curried Mint Yogurt Sauce (page 160).

Beet Purée

1 bunch of beets (about 1 pound),
washed and trimmed

3 tablespoons unsalted butter
Juice of 1/2 orange

2 tablespoons chopped chives
Sea salt and freshly ground
black pepper

Place the beets and enough water to cover in a medium saucepan and bring the water to a boil over high heat. Reduce the heat to medium, cover, and cook the beets for 30 to 35 minutes, until tender. Drain the beets, peel them, and cut them into chunks. Purée the beets in a food processor with the butter, orange juice, chives, and 2 to 3 tablespoons of the water the beets were cooked in (or more if necessary to make a smooth purée) until smooth. Season the purée to taste with salt and pepper and serve warm.

GOOD WITH: Grilled Marinated Lamb and Pepper Skewers (page 159) and Poached Chicken Breasts with Spring Vegetables and Horseradish (page 152).

Lima Bean Purée

1 pound frozen lima beans, rinsed
and drained

2 tablespoons unsalted butter

1 tablespoon olive oil

2 tablespoons chopped fresh
rosemary
Sea salt and freshly ground
black pepper

Place the lima beans in a medium saucepan with 1 tablespoon of the butter, the olive oil, and enough water to cover. Bring the water to a boil over high heat, reduce the heat to medium, cover, and cook the beans for about 20 minutes, until tender. Remove the beans with a slotted spoon, reserving the liquid, and purée them in a food processor with the remaining tablespoon butter, the rosemary, and 2 to 3 tablespoons of the water the lima beans were cooked in (or more if necessary to make a smooth purée) until smooth. Season the purée to taste with salt and pepper and serve warm.

GOOD WITH: Pan-Seared Halibut with Sautéed Sweet Peppers and Olive-Caper Relish (page 187).

mini baked potatoes

Everyone loves baked potatoes, but the giant russets that are the standard are just too big for most appetites. Now that I've begun roasting these smaller potatoes instead, I find myself serving baked potatoes much more often.

SERVES 4

. . . .

4 small Yukon Gold, red, or
California white potatoes,
gently scrubbed
Sea salt and freshly ground
black pepper

Optional toppings: olive oil or
unsalted butter; sour cream,
crème fraîche, or yogurt; finely
chopped fresh chives, scallions,
parsley, rosemary, or thyme

Preheat the oven to 400°F.

Bake the potatoes for 35 to 40 minutes, until they're soft to the squeeze and the skin is crisp. Cut a slit in the top of each potato and squeeze to push the inside of the potato upward. Sprinkle the potatoes with salt and pepper, dress them with the toppings of your choice, and serve warm.

Good with:
Pan-Grilled Beef
Fillet with Marsala
Peppercorn Sauce
(page 155), Maggie's
Curried Lamb
Chops with Curried
Mint Yogurt Sauce
(page 160), Grilled
Turkey Burgers
(page 68)

quick things to do with a bag of spinach

I try to always keep a bag of spinach on hand to use in easy recipes like these. Unless you're using baby spinach, remove the tough ends from the spinach leaves before proceeding with a recipe.

Garlic-Sautéed Spinach

SERVES 2 TO 4

Heat 1 tablespoon of olive oil in a large skillet over medium-high heat. Add 4 garlic cloves, smashed, and sauté for about 2 minutes without browning. Add the contents of a 12-ounce bag of spinach, season with salt and pepper, and toss the spinach in the skillet for 1 to 2 minutes, until it wilts. Squeeze lemon juice over the wilted spinach and sprinkle with Parmesan cheese, if desired.

Spinach-Stuffed Twice-Baked Potato

SERVES 2

Bake a large potato until soft, and split in half lengthwise. Scoop out the insides of the potato into a bowl, reserving the potato skin. Mix the potato with 1 cup of chopped Garlic-Sautéed Spinach, a few tablespoons of butter, and salt and pepper to taste. Stuff the potato mixture into the skin halves, top with grated cheese, and bake in a 400°F oven until the cheese melts.

Spinach Dip or Spread

SERVES 4

Add ½ cup of chopped Garlic-Sautéed Spinach and 2 minced scallions to 1 cup of sour cream, plain whole-milk yogurt, or softened cream cheese. Season with salt and pepper and stir to combine. Serve the dip with chips or a Crudité Platter (page 16) or spread it on bagels or sandwiches.

Scrambled Spinach and Eggs

SERVES 1

Add a handful of spinach leaves and shredded Swiss cheese or crumbled goat cheese to two to three scrambled eggs while the eggs are still runny; continue cooking until the spinach wilts and the eggs are done.

Spinach-Stuffed Chicken Breast

SERVES 1

Stuff ¼ cup of Garlic-Sautéed Spinach and a chopped garlic clove under the skin of a chicken breast. Brush the chicken with lemon juice, season with salt and pepper, and roast it in a 400°F oven for 30 to 35 minutes, until the skin is crisp and the chicken is cooked through.

Spinach and Ricotta Cheese Pasta

SERVES 4 TO 6

Cook 8 ounces of penne or ziti in a pot of salted boiling water until al dente. Reserve a cupful of the water the pasta was cooked in, drain the pasta, and immediately toss in a large bowl with the contents of a 12-ounce bag of spinach, 1 cup of fresh whole-milk ricotta cheese, and enough of the reserved water so the sauce is slippery. Season with salt and pepper and toss until the spinach wilts.

Spinach Pesto

MAKES ABOUT 1 CUP

Put the contents of a 12-ounce bag of spinach in a food processor with 1 cup parsley, ¼ cup pine nuts, 4 garlic cloves, and salt and pepper, and pulse to chop the ingredients. With the motor running, add about ⅓ cup olive oil or enough to make a smooth paste. Transfer the pesto to a bowl and stir in ½ cup freshly grated Parmesan cheese. Toss the pesto with 8 ounces of hot cooked pasta or use it as a spread for cheese toast, sandwiches, or pizza.

Greek Spinach Salad

SERVES 2 TO 4

Put the contents of a 12-ounce bag of spinach in a large bowl and add 2 chopped tomatoes, 1 chopped red or green bell pepper, 1 thinly sliced cucumber, and ⅓ cup crumbled feta cheese. Drizzle with olive oil and red wine vinegar, season with salt and pepper, and toss gently to mix.

sara says
Always give prewashed and bagged spinach and greens or vegetables one more wash before using them.

bibb wedges with radicchio, endive, and blue cheese dressing

Like most people, I grew up on the classic iceberg wedge salad. I still think it's one of the great side dishes, especially with a few new touches —like using more unusual and flavorful lettuces. I start with tender Bibb letuce and add endive and radicchio for their crunchy texture and slightly bitter flavor. Prepare this in advance because the lettuce needs time to chill and crisp in the refrigerator.

SERVES 4

BLUE CHEESE DRESSING

- ¾ cup mayonnaise
- 2 ounces crumbled blue cheese (about ½ cup)
- ¼ cup buttermilk, from a well-shaken carton
- 1 tablespoon sherry vinegar
  Sea salt and freshly ground black pepper

• • •

- 1 head of Bibb lettuce
- 1 head of radicchio
- 1 Belgian endive
- 1 ounce crumbled blue cheese (about ¼ cup)

Leaving the cores intact, cut the lettuce, radicchio, and endive into quarters through the stem ends. Soak them in a large bowl of cold water to clean them thoroughly. Drain well and wrap the quarters, a few at a time, in paper towels to dry completely. Place the wrapped quarters in plastic bags and refrigerate for at least several hours or up to overnight to chill and crisp. Chill four salad plates in the refrigerator.

To make the dressing, combine the mayonnaise, blue cheese, buttermilk, and vinegar in a blender and pulse several times, until the dressing is partially puréed with some chunks of cheese remaining. Season to taste with salt and pepper.

To serve, remove the lettuce, radicchio, endive, and salad plates from the refrigerator. Cut the cores from the lettuce, radicchio, and endive wedges, leaving the leaves of the wedges intact; discard the cores. Place one lettuce wedge, one radicchio wedge, and one endive wedge on each plate. Drizzle the dressing over the salad, top with the blue cheese, season with additional salt and pepper if desired, and serve chilled.

Good with:
Rosemary-Grilled Boneless Leg of Lamb with Tuscan White Beans and Roasted Tomatoes (page 162), Spaghetti with Quick Bolognese (page 171), or Pan-Grilled Beef Fillet with Marsala Peppercorn Sauce (page 155).

cooley tabbouleh

I gave this salad its silly name because I think tabbouleh—bulgur wheat salad loaded with fresh parsley and mint—is such a perfect, cooling side dish for a hot summer day. The bulgur is softened by soaking in water, not by cooking, so you don't even have to turn on the stove to make it.

SERVES 4 TO 6

- 1 cup bulgur wheat
  Grated zest and juice of
  3 lemons
- 2 cups chopped fresh flat-leaf parsley
- 1 bunch scallions, minced (white and green parts)
- 2 cucumbers, peeled, seeded, and chopped
- 2 tomatoes, cored and chopped
- ½ cup chopped fresh mint
- ¼ cup extra-virgin olive oil
  Sea salt and freshly ground black pepper
- 2 cups loosely packed arugula

Put the bulgur wheat in a large bowl. Combine the zest and juice of one of the lemons with 2 cups of tepid water and pour the liquid over the bulgur. Stir to mix, cover the bowl tightly with plastic wrap, and set it aside for about 30 minutes, until the bulgur has absorbed the water. Pour the bulgur into a mesh colander and press on it to extract any excess liquid.

In a separate large bowl, combine the parsley, scallions, cucumbers, tomatoes, mint, olive oil, and the zest and juice of the remaining 2 lemons and stir to combine. Add the bulgur wheat, season to taste with salt and pepper, and stir again gently. Cover the bowl, and refrigerate the tabbouleh for at least 1 hour and up to overnight before serving. Just before serving, gently toss with the arugula.

Good with:

Maggie's Curried Lamb Chops with Curried Mint Yogurt Sauce (page 160) or Grilled Vegetable "Patty Melts" with Spinach and Feta Cheese (page 78).

farmstead potato salad

I came up with this salad as a way to take advantage of all the different varieties of fingerling potatoes—Swedish Peanut, LaRatte, Purple Peruvian, and Russian Banana—that I get at the farmers' market.

SERVES 4 TO 6

. . . .

2 pounds assorted fingerling potatoes, gently scrubbed
Kosher salt

2 tablespoons sherry vinegar

CORNICHON VINAIGRETTE

2 tablespoons sherry vinegar

1 tablespoon Dijon mustard

1 tablespoon honey
Juice of half a lemon

1 shallot, minced

¼ cup extra-virgin olive oil

¼ cup canola or safflower oil

1 tablespoon chopped fresh dill

4 cornichons or mini dill pickles, minced
Sea salt and freshly ground black pepper

. . .

1 red onion, thinly sliced

2 celery stalks, diced

10 cornichons or mini dill pickles, chopped

2 tablespoons chopped fresh dill

1 tablespoon chopped fresh chives
Sea salt and freshly ground black pepper

Good With:

Grilled Turkey Burgers (page 68), Spicy Lamb Sausage Sandwiches with Roasted Peppers and Yogurt Cucumber Sauce (page 72), or Southwestern Steak Tacos with Chopped Charred Summer Vegetables (page 95).

Place the potatoes in a large pot of water and bring the water to a boil over high heat. Salt generously, reduce the heat to low, and simmer for 12 to 15 minutes, until the potatoes are tender when pierced with the tip of a knife. Drain and transfer the potatoes to a large bowl. Drizzle the potatoes with the vinegar, toss to coat, and set them aside to cool to room temperature.

To make the vinaigrette, stir the vinegar, mustard, honey, lemon juice, and shallot together in a small bowl. Gradually whisk in the oils. Stir in the dill and cornichons and season the vinaigrette to taste with salt and pepper.

Add the onion, celery, cornichons, dill, and chives to the bowl with the potatoes. Drizzle with half of the vinaigrette (or more to taste), season to taste with salt and pepper, and toss gently to mix. Serve the salad at room temperature or cover and refrigerate until ready to serve.

chickpea salad

Chickpeas, also called garbanzo beans or ceci beans, have an earthy, nutty flavor that I love. They're one of my favorite beans and also one of the foods I most readily use canned. This salad makes a nice lunch for the beach or to take to work.

SERVES 4 TO 6

. . . .

CUMIN VINAIGRETTE
- 1 tablespoon red wine vinegar
  Juice of 1 lemon
- 1 tablespoon ground cumin
- 2 garlic cloves, minced
- 2 teaspoons capers, drained
- 1 teaspoon paprika
- ½ teaspoon crushed red pepper flakes
- ¼ cup extra-virgin olive oil
  Sea salt and freshly ground black pepper

. . .

- 2 15-ounce cans chickpeas (about 3 cups), rinsed and drained
- 1 tomato, cored and chopped
- 1 roasted red bell pepper (see "Roasting Peppers," page 79; or from a jar or deli case), chopped
- 2 tablespoons fresh thyme
- 2 tablespoons chopped fresh flat-leaf parsley
  Sea salt and freshly ground black pepper
- 3 ounces feta cheese, cut into ¼-inch cubes

To make the vinaigrette, stir the vinegar, lemon juice, cumin, garlic, capers, paprika, and red pepper flakes together in a small bowl. Gradually whisk in the olive oil and season to taste with salt and pepper.

Combine the chickpeas, tomato, roasted pepper, thyme, and parsley in a separate large bowl. Drizzle with the vinaigrette, season to taste with salt and pepper, and toss to combine. Add the feta cheese and toss again gently. Serve immediately or cover and refrigerate until ready to serve.

Good with:
Grilled Steak Salad with Grilled Vegetables (page 54) or Grilled Marinated Lamb and Pepper Skewers (page 159).

classic cucumber salad

I use different herbs in this slightly sweet cucumber salad depending on what I'm serving it with.

Good with:

Pan-Seared Salmon with Sweet and Spicy Asian Glaze (page 184), CC's Lobster Tacos with Baja Fixin's (page 100), Thai-Style Sliced Beef Lettuce Wraps (page 83), or Spicy Lamb Sausage Sandwiches with Roasted Peppers and Cucumber Yogurt Sauce (page 72).

SERVES 4 TO 6

- 1 hothouse seedless cucumber, peeled in strips and thinly sliced (about 3 cups)
- 3 tablespoons white wine vinegar
- 2 tablespoons extra-virgin olive oil
- 2 tablespoons chopped fresh dill, cilantro, or mint
- Grated zest and juice of 1 lime
- 1 teaspoon sugar
- Sea salt and freshly ground black pepper

Combine the cucumber, vinegar, olive oil, dill, lime zest and juice, and sugar in a medium bowl and toss to mix. Cover the bowl and refrigerate for about 30 minutes to chill. Just before serving, season the salad to taste with salt and pepper and toss again.

spicy cole slaw

I use this slaw as a condiment on sandwiches and burgers and as a refreshing alternative to a green salad with hot entrées. Toss it just before serving so the cabbage stays nice and crunchy.

Good with:

Pan-Seared Tuna Tacos with Mango-Avocado Salsa (page 98), Grilled Turkey Burgers with Sweet Pickles (page 68), Shrimp Po'boys with Quick Herb Mayo (page 77), Grilled Focaccia Sandwich for a Crowd (page 80), Spicy Lamb Sausage Sandwiches with Roasted Peppers and Cucumber Yogurt Sauce (page 72), or Backyard Barbecued Pork Tenderloin with Baked Sweet Potatoes (page 156).

SERVES 4

- 2 cups shredded green cabbage
- 1 cup loosely packed arugula
- 10 basil leaves, thinly sliced
- 1/2 cup mayonnaise
- 1 tablespoon apple cider vinegar
- 2 teaspoons Dijon mustard
- 1 teaspoon sugar
- 1/2 teaspoon crushed red pepper flakes
- Sea salt and freshly ground black pepper

Combine the cabbage, arugula, and basil in a large bowl and refrigerate.

Whisk the mayonnaise, vinegar, mustard, sugar, and red pepper flakes together in a small bowl. Just before serving, pour the dressing over the cabbage, season to taste with salt and pepper, and toss gently to coat.

spicy black beans

Black beans have such a rich, distinctive flavor. I love them on their own, with a bowl of white rice and hot sauce. But they also make a wonderful side to grilled beef, chicken, and pork dishes like the Backyard Barbecued Pork Tenderloin with Baked Sweet Potatoes (page 156).

SERVES 4 TO 6

- 1 tablespoon olive oil
- 1 onion, diced
- 1 red bell pepper, cored, seeded, and diced
- 1 jalapeño pepper, cored, seeded, and minced
- 2 garlic cloves, minced
- 2 15-ounce cans black beans (about 3 cups), rinsed and drained
- 1 tomato, cored and diced
- 3 tablespoons chopped fresh cilantro
- 2 scallions, thinly sliced (white and green parts)
- 1 teaspoon ground cumin
  Sea salt and freshly ground black pepper

Heat the olive oil in a large skillet over medium heat. Add the onion and sauté for 3 to 4 minutes, until tender and translucent. Add the bell pepper and jalapeño pepper and sauté for 2 to 3 minutes, until the peppers are tender. Add the garlic and cook for 1 minute just to soften, stirring constantly so it doesn't brown. Add the beans, tomato, cilantro, scallions, and cumin. Stir to combine, season to taste with salt and pepper, and cook until the beans are warmed through. Serve warm.

mixed bean and sweet pepper salad

There are so many varieties of green (and not so green!) beans and peppers available at farmers' markets during the summer months, and each has its own unique flavor. I like to use as many varieties of both as I can find for this salad. It looks so pretty with the different colors and shapes adding to this line to fill out bottom line.

SERVES 4 TO 6

SHERRY VINAIGRETTE

2 tablespoons sherry vinegar

2 teaspoons Dijon mustard

Grated zest and juice of
1 lemon

½ teaspoon sugar

2 tablespoons extra-virgin olive oil

Sea salt and freshly ground
black pepper

• • •

Kosher salt

1 pound mixed beans, stem ends
removed

1 cup fresh or frozen edamame
or lima beans

2 red or yellow bell peppers,
cored, seeded, and julienned

½ pint cherry tomatoes, halved

10 fresh basil leaves, thinly sliced

2 tablespoons chopped fresh
flat-leaf parsley

2 tablespoons chopped fresh
oregano or marjoram

Sea salt and freshly ground
black pepper

To make the vinaigrette, whisk the vinegar, mustard, lemon zest and juice, and sugar together in a small bowl. Gradually whisk in the olive oil, season with salt and pepper to taste, and set aside.

Bring a medium saucepan of water to a boil and add salt. Add the green beans and edamame and blanch for 1 to 2 minutes, until they're bright colored and just tender. Drain the beans and rinse them under cold running water until they're completely cooled; drain again and pat dry.

Place the beans and edamame in a large bowl. Add the peppers, tomatoes, basil, parsley, and oregano. Drizzle the salad with the vinaigrette, season it to taste with salt and pepper, and toss to combine. Serve at room temperature or cover and refrigerate until ready to serve.

Try This!
Make this salad more substantial by dressing it with any combination of the following: torn slices of prosciutto, cubed fresh mozzarella cheese, marinated olives, or chopped celery, fennel, scallions, red onions, or roasted peppers.

Good with:
Skewered Thai Chicken Thighs with Spicy Peanut Dipping Sauce (page 150), Pan-Grilled Beef Fillet with Marsala Peppercorn Sauce (page 155), or Heirloom Tomato Tarts with Goat Cheese and Fresh Rosemary (page 109).

shell bean and pea salad with fresh mint

I make this salad in the early spring, inspired by the arrival of the first peas at my local farmers' market. I supplement the fresh peas with frozen lima beans and edamame to make it more interesting. Edamame's slightly sweet flavor and firm texture are a great addition to salads.

SERVES 4 TO 6

MINT VINAIGRETTE

- 3 tablespoons white wine vinegar
- 2 tablespoons chopped fresh mint
- 2 scallions, minced (white and green parts)
- 1 tablespoon chopped fresh chives
  Grated zest and juice of 1 lemon
- ¼ cup extra-virgin olive oil
  Sea salt and freshly ground black pepper

• • •

Kosher salt

- 1 cup fresh or frozen edamame beans
- 1 cup fresh or frozen green peas
- 1 cup fresh or frozen lima beans or fava beans
  Sea salt and freshly ground black pepper
- ⅓ cup freshly grated pecorino cheese

⚜
Good with:

Rigatoni with Sausage, Cannellini Bean, and Swiss Chard Ragù (page 118) or Pan-Seared Salmon with Sweet and Spicy Asian Glaze (page 184).

To make the vinaigrette, combine the vinegar, mint, scallions, chives, and lemon zest and juice in a small bowl and stir to mix. Gradually whisk in the olive oil, season with salt and pepper to taste, and set aside.

Bring a medium saucepan of water to a boil and add salt. Add the edamame and blanch for 1 to 2 minutes, until they're bright green and just tender. Leaving the water in the pot, use a strainer to remove the edamame and run them under cold running water until they're completely cooled. Drain them again, pat dry, and transfer to a medium bowl. Repeat the process with the peas, cooking them for about 4 minutes and adding them to the bowl with the edamame. Repeat again, cooking the lima beans for about 5 minutes and adding them to the bowl with the edamame beans and peas.

Drizzle the vinaigrette over the beans and peas, season to taste with salt and pepper, and toss to mix. Serve at room temperature or cover and refrigerate until ready to serve. Just before serving, sprinkle the pecorino cheese over the salad and toss again.

layered hoppin' john

Hoppin' John is a classic Southern side. We often eat it for lunch on New Year's day; in the South eating black-eyed peas on New Year's is believed to bring good luck. Traditionally it's served with the rice and beans mixed together, but I layer the ingredients rather than stir them together. I think it tastes—and looks—better this way.

Good with:
Shrimp Po'boys (page 77) or Pan-Seared Tuna Tacos with Mango-Avocado Salsa (page 98).

. . . .

Kosher salt

2 cups fresh or frozen black-eyed peas

1 cup long-grain white rice

Sea salt

2 tablespoons olive oil

1 red onion, diced

2 garlic cloves, minced

½ cup chopped fresh flat-leaf parsley

1 red bell pepper, cored, seeded, and diced

4 scallions, minced (white and green parts)

1 jalapeño pepper, cored, seeded, and minced

1 tablespoon fresh thyme

Freshly ground black pepper

1 cup tomato salsa (your favorite or Salsa Fresca, page 90)

4 ounces goat cheese, crumbled (about 1 cup)

¼ cup fresh cilantro leaves

Bring a medium saucepan of water to a boil and add salt. Add the black-eyed peas, lower the heat, and simmer for about 30 minutes, until they're tender. Drain the peas and transfer them to a large bowl.

Rinse the rice thoroughly in a fine-mesh strainer. Bring 1½ cups of water to a boil over high heat in a medium saucepan with a tight-fitting lid. Add the rice, season it with salt, and stir to mix. Reduce the heat, cover, and simmer over low heat for 15 to 20 minutes, until all the water is absorbed and the rice is fluffy. Turn off the heat, uncover, and fluff the rice with a fork.

While the rice is cooking, heat the oil in a large skillet over medium heat. Add the onion and sauté for 3 to 4 minutes, stirring frequently, until tender and translucent. Add the garlic and sauté for 1 minute, stirring constantly so it doesn't brown. Add the peas, parsley, bell pepper, scallions, jalapeño pepper, and thyme, and stir to mix. Season to taste with salt and pepper and sauté the vegetables over medium heat for about 3 minutes, until the peas are warmed through.

To serve, spoon the rice on a serving platter and spoon the pea mixture over the rice. Top with the salsa, then the crumbled goat cheese, and garnish with the fresh cilantro leaves.

green rice

I can appreciate plain steamed rice when I'm serving a dish with a rich sauce, but otherwise I want my side dishes to have more flavor than that. This spinach and herb-flecked rice is the answer.

SERVES 4 TO 6

Good with:

Grilled Marinated Lamb and Pepper Skewers (page 159) or Curried Chicken Sauté (page 147).

Try This!

When you want a touch of sweetness, add chopped tomatoes or roasted red pepper strips along with the parsley. Or stir in a cup of canned black beans, rinsed and drained, and top the rice with fresh tomato salsa.

sara says

After adding the vegetables, stir the rice only once to prevent it from getting sticky.

1 cup long-grain white rice

1 tablespoon olive oil

1 onion, diced
Sea salt

1 cup fresh or frozen green peas (preferably petite peas)

1½ cups loosely packed spinach, washed, drained, and trimmed of tough stems

¼ cup chopped fresh flat-leaf parsley

4 scallions, thinly sliced (white and green parts)
Grated zest and juice of 1 lemon
Freshly ground black pepper

Rinse the rice thoroughly in a fine-mesh strainer and drain it well.

Heat the oil in a medium saucepan over medium heat. Add the onion and sauté for 3 to 4 minutes, until tender and translucent. Add the rice, season it with salt, and cook and stir for about 2 minutes. Add 1½ cups of cold water and stir to mix, making sure to release any rice stuck to the pan. Bring the water to a low boil, reduce the heat to low, and simmer, covered, for about 10 minutes. Add the peas and continue to simmer for about 5 minutes, until all the water is absorbed and the rice is fluffy.

Remove the pot from the heat, add the spinach, cover, and let it sit for about 2 minutes, until the spinach wilts. Add the parsley, scallions, and lemon zest and juice. Season to taste with salt and pepper, stir gently to combine, and serve warm.

lemon-coconut basmati rice pilaf

Cooking rice with coconut milk makes it rich and slightly sweet.

SERVES 4 TO 6

. . . .

1½ cups basmati rice
  1 tablespoon unsalted butter
  1 tablespoon olive oil
  1 onion, chopped
    Sea salt
  2 cups chicken or vegetable broth
    or water
  ½ cup unsweetened coconut milk,
    from a well-shaken can

Grated zest and juice of 1 lemon
Freshly ground black pepper
  ½ cup chopped fresh herbs
    (cilantro, parsley, oregano,
    marjoram, chives, or a
    combination)

Good with:
Skewered Thai
Chicken Thighs
with Spicy Peanut
Dipping Sauce
(page 150), Curried
Chicken Sauté
(page 147), Grilled
Marinated Lamb
and Pepper Skewers
(page 159), or
Pan-Seared Sea
Scallops with Corn
Coulis (page 183).

Rinse the rice thoroughly in a fine mesh strainer and drain it well.

Heat the butter and the olive oil in a medium saucepan over medium heat until hot. Add the onion and sauté for 3 to 4 minutes, until tender and translucent. Add the rice, season it with salt, and cook and stir for about 2 minutes. Add the broth, coconut milk, lemon zest and juice, and pepper and stir to combine. Bring to a low boil, reduce the heat to low, cover, and simmer for 15 to 20 minutes, until all the liquid is absorbed and the rice is fluffy. Remove the saucepan from the heat, add the herbs, and stir gently to combine. Season with additional salt and pepper if desired and serve warm.

simplest
sweets

Fluffy Dark Chocolate Mousse

Individual Tartes Tatins

Individual Peach-Raspberry Crostatas

Grilled Apricots with Buttermilk
Ice Cream

Caramelized Bananas Foster Splits

Blueberry Cornmeal Pancakes with
Maple Caramel Sauce

Lemon Poached Pears with
Lemon Cream

Ten Easy, Elegant Parfaits

Cherries Jubilee with Vanilla Frozen
Yogurt

Frozen Layered Terrine

Ice Cream Fondue with
Warm Dark Chocolate Sauce and
Warm Raspberry Sauce

Bittersweet Chocolate Pudding

Brownie Mocha Latte Sundaes

IF, LIKE ME, you lack the patience and precision necessary to bake cakes and such, the desserts in this chapter are for you. Making them is more like cooking than baking, in that these recipes rely on good ingredients—ripe, seasonal fruit, quality chocolate, and premium ice cream—and only the simplest techniques. These desserts—sweet summer apricots marinated in balsamic vinegar and cooked on the grill, cherries stewed in red wine and served with store-bought frozen yogurt, and the best-quality bittersweet chocolate transformed into a deeply rich version of old-fashioned chocolate pudding—can be made at the last minute and with very little effort. Unlike technical baking recipes, none of these will fall apart if you change them a bit, which I urge you to do: substitute one fruit that's in season for another or use different flavors of ice cream in a sundae. These recipes are nearly impossible to mess up. This is dessert *my* way.

fluffy dark chocolate mousse

This mousse couldn't be any lighter. It's a good dessert to serve company since it can be made several days in advance.

SERVES 6 TO 8; MAKES ABOUT 4 CUPS

· ·

6 ounces good-quality semisweet chocolate (such as Scharffen Berger or Valrhona), finely chopped

8 tablespoons (1 stick) unsalted butter

3 large eggs, separated

¼ cup sugar

½ cup heavy cream

1 teaspoon pure vanilla extract

Unsweetened whipped cream

Additional semisweet chocolate for shaving

Melt the chocolate and butter together in the top of a double boiler over medium-low heat or in a metal bowl placed over (but not touching) simmering water, stirring occasionally. Lightly beat the egg yolks and slowly whisk into the chocolate mixture. Stir the mixture over low heat for 3 to 4 minutes. Set aside to cool to room temperature.

Beat the egg whites in a large bowl with an electric mixer on high speed until soft peaks form. Add the sugar and continue beating just until stiff peaks form.

In a separate medium bowl, whip the heavy cream with an electric mixer on high speed until soft peaks form. Add the vanilla and continue whipping until stiff peaks form.

Fold one-third of the whipped cream into the chocolate mixture with a rubber spatula. (This lightens the chocolate and makes it easier to incorporate into the other ingredients.) Add the chocolate–whipped cream mixture and the remaining whipped cream to the bowl with the egg whites and fold gently until the ingredients are just combined but still slightly marbled. (For a light, fluffy mouse, it's better to have marbling than to mix it more than necessary.) Cover and refrigerate the mousse for at least 3 hours or up to several days. To serve, divide the chilled mousse among six wineglasses. Top with a dollop of the whipped cream and chocolate shavings.

sara says

To make chocolate shavings, use a vegetable peeler to shave the chocolate from a bar or chunk.

Do not overbeat egg whites or they will break into grainy clumps.

individual tartes tatin

Tarte tatin is the French version of apple pie. They're delicious with cinnamon-spiced whipped cream or vanilla ice cream, or with eggnog poured over and around them.

SERVES 6

. . . .

1 sheet of frozen puff pastry (such as Pepperidge Farm or Dufour's), thawed in the refrigerator
All-purpose flour for dusting the work surface

3 tart apples, such as Granny Smith or Pippin
1 lemon, halved
1 cup sugar

Place six 8-ounce ovenproof ramekins on a rimmed baking sheet.

Roll out the puff pastry on a lightly floured work surface, just enough to iron out the creases. Cut out six rounds slightly larger than the ramekins, place the pastry rounds on a baking sheet, and chill.

Peel the apples and halve them crosswise. Place the halves in a small bowl and squeeze the lemon juice over them to prevent discoloring.

Cook but do not stir the sugar in a medium saucepan over medium-high heat for 4 to 5 minutes, swirling the pan continuously until the sugar dissolves and turns a dark amber color. Carefully pour the caramel into the bottoms of the ramekins, dividing it evenly, and place one apple half cut side down in each ramekin. Remove the pastry from the refrigerator and place one pastry round over each apple half, tucking the edges inside the ramekin. Chill for about 15 minutes before baking.

Preheat the oven to 400°F.

Bake the tarts from the refrigerator for 20 to 25 minutes, until the crusts are golden brown and the caramel is bubbling around the edges. Place the tarts on a wire rack for about 3 minutes to cool slightly, then run a knife around the edges of the tarts to release them from the ramekins. Place a small dessert plate on top of each ramekin and invert the tarts onto the plates. (Don't wait longer than a few minutes to remove them or the caramel will harden onto the ramekins.) Serve warm.

sara says
I don't remove the seeds or core from these apples. It takes so much time and it's no trouble to just eat around them.

individual peach-raspberry crostatas

Crostata is the Italian name for a free-form tart—one made without a tart pan. The edges of the crust are folded over the fruit to hold in the juices. When we make them at the Market, people love to buy them to take to friends because they're really beautiful in a rustic, homemade way.

SERVES 8

. . . .

FOR THE CRUST

- 2 cups all-purpose flour, plus extra for dusting the work surface
- 3 tablespoons sugar
- ¼ teaspoon kosher or sea salt
- ½ pound (2 sticks) cold unsalted butter, cut into cubes, plus extra for greasing the baking sheet
- 1 large egg yolk
- 3 to 4 tablespoons ice-cold milk or ice water

FOR THE FILLING

- 2 pounds peaches, peeled, pitted, and thinly sliced
- 1 cup fresh raspberries
- ⅓ cup sugar, plus extra for sprinkling
- 3 tablespoons cornstarch
- ½ teaspoon ground cinnamon
- ¼ teaspoon ground ginger
- ¼ teaspoon kosher or sea salt
- 4 tablespoons (½ stick) unsalted butter, cut into 8 pieces
- 1 large egg
- 1 to 2 tablespoons milk

Good With:
Vanilla ice cream or Buttermilk Ice Cream (page 231), whipped cream, or frozen yogurt.

To make the crust, stir the flour, sugar, and salt together in a large bowl. Add the butter and blend it in with the flour using a pastry blender or two knives in a crisscrossing motion until the mixture resembles coarse meal. Whisk the egg yolk and 3 tablespoons of the milk together in a small bowl, add it to the flour mixture, and stir until the dough just comes together and starts to form a ball, adding the remaining tablespoon of milk if necessary. Dust your hands lightly with flour and press the dough together to form a flat round disk. Cover the dough with plastic wrap and place it in the refrigerator to chill for at least 1 hour or overnight.

Lightly grease two large baking sheets or cover with parchment and set aside.

To make the filling, combine the peaches, raspberries, sugar, cornstarch, cinnamon, ginger, and salt in a large bowl and stir gently to mix.

Remove the dough from the refrigerator and cut it into eight equal-size pieces. Lightly flour your work surface and roll each piece of dough into a 6-inch round. Place the rounds on the prepared baking sheets.

Scoop the filling and all the juices into the center of each round, dividing it evenly and leaving a 1-inch border around the edge of each tart. Place one piece of butter on top of each mound of fruit. Fold the dough over the fruit all the way around each tart to form an edge.

Whisk the egg and milk together in a small bowl to form an egg wash and brush it onto the edges of each tart. Sprinkle sugar over the egg wash and put the tarts in the refrigerator for about 30 minutes to chill.

Preheat the oven to 375°F.

Remove the tarts from the refrigerator and bake for 40 to 45 minutes, rotating the baking sheets halfway through, until the crusts are golden brown and the fruit is bubbling. Leave the tarts on the pan to cool slightly and serve warm.

Try This!

Make crostatas using whatever fruit or combinations are in season: pear-raspberry, apple, Italian plum, mixed berry, or rhubarb.

grilled apricots with buttermilk ice cream

In the summertime, when apricots (and other stone fruit) are in season, simply grilling them to intensify their sweetness makes a delicious dessert. You want the fruit to be ripe and juicy, but not so mushy that it will fall apart on the grill.

SERVES 4

. . . .

2 tablespoons balsamic vinegar

2 tablespoons honey, plus extra for drizzling

6 apricots, halved and pitted

1 pint Buttermilk Ice Cream (recipe follows) or vanilla ice cream

Prepare a hot fire in a charcoal or gas grill.

Stir the vinegar and honey together in a shallow bowl. Add the apricots and turn to coat. Place the apricots cut side down on the grill for about 4 minutes per side, turning once and brushing with the reserved vinegar-honey while they cook, until grill marks appear.

To serve, place three apricot halves on each plate, top with a scoop of ice cream, and drizzle with honey.

Try This!
You can grill any ripe, seasonal fruit just as you would the apricots: pineapple, mango, plums, nectarines, or peaches. Or season the fruit with sea salt and freshly ground black pepper before grilling and serve them alongside grilled pork chops or pork tenderloin. You can also use a grill pan if you like.

BUTTERMILK ICE CREAM
Makes about 1 quart

1½ cups buttermilk, well shaken
1 cup heavy cream
½ cup sugar
3 large egg yolks
1 tablespoon pure vanilla extract
Pinch of kosher or sea salt

Whisk the buttermilk, cream, sugar, egg yolks, vanilla, and salt together in a medium heavy-bottomed saucepan and cook the mixture over very low heat for 8 to 10 minutes, stirring constantly, until it's thick enough to coat the back of a spoon. Transfer the mixture to a bowl, cover, and chill for at least 2 hours.

Pour the ice cream mixture into an ice cream maker and freeze it according to the manufacturer's instructions for 25 to 30 minutes, until it's the consistency of soft-serve ice cream. For hard ice cream, transfer it to an airtight container to freeze for several more hours.

caramelized bananas foster splits

Bananas Foster, a classic dessert invented at Brennan's restaurant in New Orleans, is a dessert made from bananas caramelized with sugar and rum and served with ice cream. Here, I turned the bananas into a decadent banana split sundae using dulce de leche ice cream, which I think is the best thing to happen to ice cream since vanilla. Start with bananas that are ripe, but not overripe, dark, or speckled.

SERVES 4

. . . .

4 tablespoons (½ stick) unsalted butter

2 ripe bananas, peeled and halved lengthwise

½ cup packed light brown sugar

¼ cup dark rum

½ cup heavy cream

1 pint dulce de leche ice cream
Salted Spanish peanuts, lightly toasted (optional)

Heat the butter in a large skillet over medium-high heat until hot. Place the bananas cut side down in the skillet and sauté for about 2 minutes, until light brown. Carefully turn the bananas, sprinkle with the brown sugar, and cook for another minute, shaking the pan constantly to prevent the sugar from burning. Remove the bananas and place one banana half in each of four dessert bowls.

Add the rum to the skillet, stir to mix, and bring it to a boil over high heat. Continue to boil the rum for about 1 minute to burn off the alcohol and reduce it slightly. Add the cream and simmer for 2 to 3 minutes, stirring constantly, until the sugar dissolves and the sauce thickens.

To serve, scoop the ice cream over the bananas, spoon the sauce on top, and sprinkle the sundaes with the peanuts, if you're using them.

blueberry cornmeal pancakes with maple caramel sauce

Pancakes for dessert are so unexpected and people love them. This recipe came about as a way for me to turn fresh sweet blueberries into dessert for company—without turning on the oven.

SERVES 4 TO 6

. . . .

¾ cup all-purpose flour

½ cup yellow cornmeal

2 tablespoons granulated sugar

2 teaspoons baking powder

½ teaspoon baking soda

½ teaspoon ground cinnamon

Pinch of kosher or sea salt

2 large eggs, separated

1 cup buttermilk, from a well-shaken carton

3 tablespoons unsalted butter, melted, plus more for the pan

1 teaspoon pure vanilla extract

2 tablespoons light brown sugar

1 cup blueberries

Maple Caramel Sauce (recipe follows)

🍂
Quick Fix:
Use pancake mix instead of making the batter from scratch. The blueberries and maple sauce will make them special.

Stir the flour, cornmeal, granulated sugar, baking powder, baking soda, cinnamon, and salt together in a large bowl. In a medium bowl, whisk the egg yolks, buttermilk, butter, and vanilla together.

In a third medium bowl, beat the egg whites with an electric mixer on high speed or a wire whisk until soft peaks form.

Add the egg-buttermilk mixture to the flour mixture and stir to combine thoroughly. Gently fold in the egg whites until they're just combined.

Heat a griddle or a large skillet over medium-high heat until hot. Spread about a tablespoon of butter evenly over the griddle.

Make 2 or 3 pancakes, using about 1 tablespoon of the batter for each. Cook them for 2 to 3 minutes, until bubbles appear over their surface. Sprinkle a pinch of the brown sugar and a few blueberries on each pancake, flip, and cook for about 2 minutes on the second side, until they're golden brown. Transfer the pancakes to a plate and cover them loosely with foil to keep them warm while you cook the remaining pancakes.

Serve the pancakes drizzled with the warm Maple Caramel Sauce and the remaining blueberries scattered over the top.

*sara says*___
For light, fluffy pancakes do not mix the batter any more than necessary.

❧
Try This!
Serve these for
breakfast topped
with even more
fresh blueberries
and maple syrup.

MAPLE CARAMEL SAUCE

Makes 1 cup

1 cup pure maple syrup
1 tablespoon pure vanilla extract
2 tablespoons heavy cream

Bring the maple syrup and vanilla to a boil in a medium saucepan over medium heat. Reduce the heat to low and simmer the syrup for about 3 minutes, stirring occasionally, until it's thick. Remove the sauce from the heat and stir in the cream.

lemon poached pears with lemon cream

Poached pears may seem esoteric, but I've never served them where they weren't a big hit. These are poached long enough for the pears to absorb the poaching liquid, giving them a tender and buttery texture.

SERVES 4

. . . .

1 lemon
1 750 ml bottle dry white wine
  (about 3½ cups)
1 cup sugar
¼ cup dark rum

8 whole cloves
  Pinch of kosher or sea salt
1 vanilla bean
4 Bosc pears, peeled
  Lemon Cream (recipe follows)

sara says____
*Bosc pears hold
their shape best
when cooked,
but if you can't
find them, any
variety will do.*

Zest the lemon using a citrus zester or cut off the zest and cut it into very thin strips.

Place the lemon zest in a medium saucepan with the wine, sugar, rum, cloves, and salt. Cut the lemon in half and squeeze the juice into the saucepan. Split the vanilla bean in half, scrape the seeds into the saucepan, then drop the split bean into the saucepan. Bring the mixture to a low boil over medium-high heat, stirring occasionally. Add the pears. If the liquid in the pan doesn't cover them, add up to 1 cup of water to just cover the pears. (If the pears still are not covered, transfer them to a smaller saucepan rather than adding more water.) Cover the pan and reduce the heat and simmer the pears for 25 to 30 minutes, until tender. Use a slotted spoon to lift the pears from the liquid onto a plate and cover them loosely with foil to keep warm. Return the liquid to a low boil, reduce the heat, and simmer for about 30 minutes, until it reduces and thickens to a syrupy consistency.

Place one pear on each of four plates. Drizzle with the poaching liquid, dollop a spoonful of the Lemon Cream next to each pear, and serve the remaining Lemon Cream on the side.

LEMON CREAM
Makes about 2 cups

1 cup heavy cream
¼ cup prepared lemon curd (your favorite)

Whip the heavy cream in a medium bowl with an electric mixer on high speed until soft peaks form. Gently fold in the lemon curd. Serve immediately or refrigerate in an airtight container until ready to serve.

ten easy, elegant parfaits

Parfaits are just the kind of dessert I like to make—they're fast, they take advantage of the natural flavor of fresh fruit, and (best of all) they don't require baking. I don't follow any rules when I make parfaits. I build them with whatever fruit is in season—or whatever other ingredients I have on hand. Here are some combinations I like:

Simple Strawberry Parfaits (*pictured opposite*)

Sprinkle a pint of sliced strawberries with $\frac{1}{2}$ cup of sugar, the grated zest and juice of 1 orange, and 1 tablespoon balsamic vinegar and set aside for 15 minutes. Whip 1 cup of heavy cream with $\frac{1}{2}$ cup sugar until soft peaks form. Starting with the fruit and ending with whipped cream, make 3 layers in each of 4 dessert glasses.

Ricotta Cheese, Walnut, and Honey Parfaits

Stir enough heavy cream or milk into 2 cups fresh ricotta cheese to obtain a soft consistency. Starting with the ricotta cheese, build the parfait in three layers, drizzling each layer with honey and sprinkling lightly toasted walnuts over each layer of honey.

Pineapple Caramel Sundae Parfaits

Sprinkle 2 cups chopped pineapple with a few spoonfuls of brown sugar to sweeten the fruit to taste. Stir a pint of vanilla frozen yogurt until soft. Starting with the pineapple, layer the pineapple and frozen yogurt in four glasses and drizzle them with prepared caramel sauce.

Jell-O Parfaits

Prepare cherry or raspberry Jell-O according to package instructions and pour into four glasses. Add mixed berries, sliced strawberries, or diced pineapple and refrigerate until the Jell-O is firm. Top with a dollop of whipped cream or crème fraîche and a scattering of the fruit you've made it with.

Raspberry Chocolate-Brownie Ice Cream Parfait

Sprinkle a few spoonfuls of sugar over 2 cups raspberries to sweeten them to taste. Stir 1 pint chocolate ice cream until soft, then stir in one crumbled brownie. Starting with the berries, layer the berries and ice cream mixture in four glasses and top with shaved or grated dark chocolate.

Try This!

Create strawberry shortcake parfaits by layering thin slices of pound cake or angel food cake, or crisp butter cookies, into these parfaits.

Lemon Cream and Plum Parfaits

Sprinkle a few spoonfuls of sugar and the juice of half an orange over 2 cups chopped peeled plums to sweeten the plums to taste. Whip 1 cup heavy cream until stiff peaks form and fold in ¼ cup lemon curd. Starting with the plums, layer the plums and the lemon curd cream in four glasses, ending with a dollop of the cream.

Mixed Berry–Crème Fraîche Parfaits

Sprinkle a few spoonfuls of sugar over 1 cup blueberries and 1 cup raspberries to sweeten the berries to taste. Add the grated zest and juice of 1 lemon and let the berries sit for about 5 minutes. Whip 1 cup crème fraîche with ¼ cup sour cream until fluffy. Starting with the berries, layer the berries and crème fraîche mixture in four glasses and chill until ready to serve.

Ambrosia Parfaits

Sprinkle a few spoonfuls of sugar over 2 cups orange and grapefruit wedges (with their juices) to sweeten the fruit to taste. Starting with the citrus wedges, layer the wedges with whipped cream and coconut flakes in four glasses. Top with a scoop of marshmallow fluff and fresh or Maraschino cherries.

All-Chocolate Parfaits with Chocolate Sandwich Cookies

Stir chocolate ice cream to soften. Starting with the ice cream, layer the ice cream with chocolate sandwich cookies (two cookies in each parfait) in four glasses, and drizzle each layer of cookie with chocolate sauce (see Warm Dark Chocolate Sauce, page 245). Top with a dollop of whipped cream and chocolate chips, chunks, or shavings.

Italian Peach and Mascarpone Parfaits

Pour 2 tablespoons vin santo (Italian dessert wine or any dessert wine) and sprinkle a few spoonfuls of sugar over 2 cups chopped or sliced peeled peaches. Whip ½ cup heavy cream until stiff peaks form. Fold in 1 cup mascarpone cheese and ¼ cup sugar. Starting with the peaches, layer the peaches with the mascarpone mixture in four glasses and top with crumbled amaretti cookies or ginger snaps.

cherries jubilee with vanilla frozen yogurt

This is a classic. I make it with frozen yogurt instead of ice cream because I like the tanginess of the yogurt with the sweet, syrupy cherries. Use any variety of cherries you want—sweet or sour.

SERVES 4 TO 6

- 2 cups pitted cherries (about 10 ounces), plus extra for garnish
- ¾ cup dry white wine
- ½ cup packed light brown sugar
- Juice of 1 orange
- 2 tablespoons brandy or bourbon
- 1 pint vanilla frozen yogurt

Combine the cherries, wine, brown sugar, orange juice, and brandy in a small saucepan and bring to a boil over medium-high heat. Reduce the heat to low and simmer the cherries for about 20 minutes, stirring occasionally, until the sauce thickens to a syrupy consistence. Remove the cherries from the heat and set aside for 10 to 15 minutes to cool slightly.

To serve, divide the yogurt among four to six dessert bowls, spoon the warm sauce and cherries over the yogurt, and top each serving with a few fresh cherries.

frozen layered terrine

This is the perfect make-ahead dessert, but it takes some planning. It's made by refreezing packaged ice cream into a loaf pan. Each layer has to be frozen before another layer is added and then the terrine must be frozen a final time for at least 8 hours. This terrine technique lends itself to endless variations and combinations of ice cream and sorbet. The berry sorbet and ice cream combination is pictured opposite. If you want, dress up a slice of the terrine as you would a scoop of ice cream, with a drizzle of sauce and crispy butter cookies on the side.

SERVES 6 TO 8

. . . .

- 3 pints of ice cream, frozen yogurt, or sorbet, in any of the following combinations:

- Raspberry sorbet, strawberry ice cream, and blueberry, blackberry, or boysenberry sorbet

- Coffee ice cream, rocky road ice cream, and chocolate ice cream or sorbet

- Mango sorbet, pineapple sorbet, and banana ice cream or sorbet

- Mango sorbet, raspberry sorbet, and lemon or lime sorbet

- Dulce de leche ice cream, pralines and cream ice cream, and butter pecan ice cream

- Pistachio ice cream, chocolate ice cream, and strawberry ice cream

- Cherry ice cream, vanilla fudge ice cream, and vanilla ice cream

- Strawberry cheesecake ice cream, strawberry ice cream, and strawberry sorbet

Place a 9 x 5 x 3-inch loaf pan in the freezer for about 30 minutes until it's ice cold. Remove one pint of ice cream from the freezer to soften it to a spreadable consistency, about 10 minutes (or soften it in the microwave for about 30 seconds).

Spread the first flavor in an even layer on the bottom of the loaf pan. Place a sheet of plastic wrap on top and press it into the corners of the pan. Freeze for about 45 minutes, until firm.

Remove the second ice cream flavor from the freezer and soften it to a spreadable consistency. Remove the terrine from the freezer, remove the plastic wrap, and spread the second pint in an even layer. Place a clean sheet of plastic wrap on top and freeze for about 45 minutes, until firm.

Repeat the process with the remaining pint. Cover the terrine with a clean sheet of plastic wrap and freeze for 8 hours or overnight.

About an hour before serving, place the pan in a bath of warm water that comes to just below the rim for about 1 minute. Remove the pan from the water and run a knife around the inside edges to loosen the terrine. Place a large sheet of plastic wrap on a work surface and invert the terrine onto the plastic. Wrap the the terrine in plastic and return it to the freezer for about 1 hour to firm completely before serving. To serve, unwrap the terrine and cut it into $1/2$-inch-thick slices.

Good with:

Warm Dark Chocolate Sauce or Warm Raspberry Sauce (page 245).

ice cream fondue with warm dark chocolate sauce and warm raspberry sauce

There's no doubt that people like to play with their food, which is why fondue is always a dinner party hit. In this version, the "dippers" are chunks of ice cream, frozen into bite-size squares and served with dessert sauces. *See photograph on page 222.*

SERVES 4 TO 6

. . . .

✿
Quick Fix:
Use a good-quality jarred chocolate sauce in place of the Warm Dark Chocolate Sauce.

1 pint vanilla, chocolate, or coffee ice cream
Warm Dark Chocolate Sauce (recipe follows)

Warm Raspberry Sauce (recipe follows)

Cut the ice cream carton away from the ice cream and peel away and discard the carton. Stand the block of ice cream vertically on a piece of waxed paper or plastic wrap and cut it into thirds. Cut the sections crosswise into roughly 1-inch cubes. Place the ice cream cubes in a single layer in a plastic or glass dish lined with waxed paper or plastic wrap, cover, and return the ice cream to the freezer to firm for at least 1 hour or overnight.

At least 30 minutes before serving, place a glass or ceramic serving bowl in the freezer to chill.

Just before serving, remove the ice cream and the serving bowl from the freezer. Spike each ice cream cube with a toothpick and place the cubes in the chilled bowl. Serve immediately, with bowls of the Warm Dark Chocolate Sauce and Warm Raspberry Sauce for guests to dip the ice cream into.

WARM DARK CHOCOLATE SAUCE
Makes 2 cups

1 cup heavy cream
½ cup dark corn syrup
**5 ounces good-quality semisweet
   chocolate, finely chopped**
**5 ounces good-quality bittersweet
   chocolate, finely chopped**

Combine the heavy cream and corn syrup in a small heavy-bottomed saucepan over medium heat and bring to a low boil. Add the semisweet and bittersweet chocolates, reduce the heat, and stir until the chocolate has melted. Remove the sauce from the heat and serve immediately or cover and refrigerate until ready to serve.

WARM RASPBERRY SAUCE
Makes 1 cup

1 pint fresh raspberries
1 cup sugar
**2 tablespoons raspberry liqueur or
   orange liqueur**
Grated zest and juice of 1 orange

Combine the raspberries, sugar, liqueur, and orange zest and juice in a small saucepan and bring to a boil over medium-high heat. Reduce the heat and simmer for about 5 minutes, until the sauce has reduced and thickened slightly. Pass the sauce through a fine-mesh strainer and discard the solids. Serve immediately or cover and refrigerate until ready to serve.

sara says———
Always use a good-quality chocolate, such as Scharffen Berger or Valrhona.

Quick Fix:
Reheat the chocolate sauce over medium heat, stirring constantly, or in a microwave for about 1 minute, stirring several times.

bittersweet chocolate pudding

Everyone has the dessert that was her childhood favorite. Mine was chocolate pudding. This is a super-rich, super-dark version of the old-fashioned pudding my mom used to make. I like it best when it's still slightly warm, but it can also be served chilled.

SERVES 6

. . . .

- 6 ounces good-quality bittersweet chocolate (such as Scharffen Berger or Valrhona), finely chopped
- 2 cups heavy cream
- 3 tablespoons sugar
  Pinch of kosher or sea salt
- 4 large egg yolks, lightly beaten
- 1 tablespoon pure vanilla extract
  Whipped cream

sara says
This pudding is really bitter-sweet. If you like it a little more sweet, add a few more tablespoons of sugar.

Preheat the oven to 325°F. Place six 4-ounce ramekins on a rimmed baking sheet and set aside.

Melt the chocolate with ½ cup of the cream in the top of a double boiler over medium-low heat or in a metal bowl placed over (but not touching) simmering water, stirring occasionally. Remove the chocolate from the heat and stir until the mixture is smooth.

Bring the remaining 1½ cups of cream to a simmer in a small saucepan over low heat, stirring occasionally, and simmer until the cream is scalded (a light skin will have formed on top). Stir in the sugar and salt, remove from the heat, and continue stirring until the sugar dissolves.

Add the hot cream to the chocolate mixture and whisk until the mixture is smooth. Slowly whisk the egg yolks into the chocolate mixture, return the mixture to the double boiler, and cook it over low heat (the water should be simmering), stirring constantly, for 3 to 4 minutes.

Pour the pudding into the ramekins, dividing it evenly. Cover each ramekin with foil and bake the puddings for 15 to 18 minutes, until the edges are slightly firm but the centers are still soft and jiggle when you shake the pan. Uncover the puddings and place them on a rack to cool for at least 1 hour. If serving warm, dollop the whipped cream on top of the pudding; otherwise, let the puddings cool completely, then cover and refrigerate them until ready to serve. Top with the whipped cream just before serving.

brownie mocha latte sundaes

When I got a cappuccino maker, I went crazy steaming milk for everything from hot cereal to sundaes. This is a hybrid of a mocha latte and a brownie sundae. The steamed milk and espresso soften the brownie so it becomes pudding-like in the bottom of the glass. If you don't have a milk steamer, bring the milk to a rolling boil in a saucepan and whisk it to make it a bit foamy.

SERVES 4

. . . .

4 2-inch-square brownies
1 pint coffee ice cream
1 cup hot brewed espresso or strong coffee
1 cup whole milk, steamed
¼ cup Warm Dark Chocolate Sauce (page 245) or good-quality chocolate sauce

Unsweetened whipped cream (optional)
Good-quality semisweet chocolate (such as Scharffen Berger or Valrhona) for shaving

Try This!

Use coffee liqueur, hazelnut syrup, or caramel sauce in place of the Warm Dark Chocolate Sauce in this recipe. Or use hot chocolate instead of coffee with steamed milk.

Place the brownies in the microwave for about 15 seconds to warm them. (Or wrap them in foil and place them in a 350°F oven for about 10 minutes.)

Put each brownie in a dessert bowl or large coffee cup. Top with the ice cream, dividing it evenly, and pour ¼ cup of the espresso and ¼ cup of the steamed milk over each serving. Drizzle each of the sundaes with 1 tablespoon of the Warm Dark Chocolate Sauce. Top with the whipped cream if you are using it, then use a vegetable peeler to shave chocolate over each serving and serve warm.

acknowledgments

· ·

I WANT TO EXPRESS MY GRATITUDE to all the people who supported my first two books, *The Foster's Market Cookbook* and *Fresh Every Day.* Your positive responses at signings and special functions and via e-mails planted the seeds for this book, and your continuous feedback helped shape it as it came to life. Of course, I must also thank the customers who continue to support Foster's Markets in every way through eating and shopping, both in the store and online. The daily contact with so many diverse people whose opinions I respect has been an amazing source of information, ideas, and inspiration over the years. Through you all I've come to really understand the kind of food you want: fast, easy, and fresh tasting.

I also want to thank the team that put this book together. We collaborated much like a restaurant staff. We were such a small crew that we all did a bit of everything.

- Thanks to Carolynn Carreño, my coauthor, for her complete understanding of my food philosophy and cooking style and her tireless dedication to put it all into the right words. She makes me focus and think about things from many different angles, always for the better.

- Thanks to Quentin Bacon, a brilliant photographer, for making my food appear on the page the way food really looks. He gives so much life to the page that you want to take a bite out of it. Thanks also to Quentin for his patience and guidance. He not only functions as a photographer but also steps in as impromptu art director, food stylist, prop stylist, and much more.

- Thanks to Pam Krauss, my editor, and Lauren Shakely, for being behind this project since its conception—and even before. Pam's talent and expertise made this book a more concentrated, vibrant version of itself than it would have been otherwise. And thanks also to Chalkley Calderwood Pratt for the beautiful design and Jane Treuhaft, and the entire team at Clarkson Potter that packages and markets the book so passionately.

- Thanks to Wendy Goldstein for testing the recipes and styling the food with such an impeccable attention to detail. Her boundless energy makes long days seem shorter. Thanks to William Smith for styling the food with such ease, and for always knowing where to buy the best of anything in New York; Lauren Volo in Quentin's office for flawlessly organizing our photo shoots; Marina Maulchin for understanding the casual style of this book and supplying the props to reflect this. And thanks to all the Foster's Market staff and my friends, family, and neighbors who share their recipes with me and give me feedback on my recipes—an invaluable tool in writing easy recipes that really work.

- Thanks to my agent, Janis Donnaud, who continues to believe in me and my food.

- And lastly, thanks to all the growers, farmers, and purveyors who work so hard every day to bring us great fresh products to work with. It's to you that I owe the most gratitude. Your dedication and those delicious raw materials encourage me—and I think all of us—to eat better and to cook better every day.

index

• •

Note: **Boldfaced** page references
indicate photographs.